HANDBOOK OF
Irish
ANTIQUITIES

St. Doulough's Church, Co. Dublin.

HANDBOOK OF
Irísh
ANTIQUITIES

William F. Wakeman

BRACKEN BOOKS
LONDON

Handbook of Irish Antiquities

First published in 1891 by
Hodges, Figgis and Co., Grafton Street, Dublin

This edition published in 1995 by Bracken Books, an imprint of
Studio Editions Ltd, Princess House, 50 Eastcastle Street,
London W1N 7AP, England

ISBN 1 85891 256 3
Printed and bound in Guernsey by
The Guernsey Press Co Ltd

IF THE BULWARKS

OF

IRISH HISTORY AND ARCHÆOLOGY

HAVE AT LENGTH BEEN RENDERED STAUNCH AND STRONG

AGAINST ASSAULTS

OF

IGNORANCE OR ERROR,

THE RESULT IS MAINLY OWING TO THE WELL-DIRECTED

LEARNING, ENERGY, AND GENIUS

OF THAT BAND OF THINKERS AND WORKERS, AMONGST WHOM

THE LATE

GEORGE PETRIE, LL.D.,

JOHN O'DONOVAN, LL.D.,

AND

JAMES HENTHORN TODD, D.D.,

WERE CAPTAINS.

TO

THE RIGHT REV. CHARLES GRAVES, D.D.,
Bishop of Limerick;

AND

THE RIGHT REV. WILLIAM REEVES, D.D.,
Bishop of Down and Connor and Dromore;

SOLE SURVIVORS OF THAT GIFTED COMPANY,

This little Work

IS RESPECTFULLY DEDICATED BY

THE AUTHOR.

PREFACE.

THE year 1848, what may be styled a precursor of my present "Handbook of Irish Antiquities" was published. Since then a new impulse, leading to the study of Archæology in this country, has, for various reasons, steadily prevailed. In the first place, our antiquarian writers, as a rule, no longer propounded the visionary theories of an older school. Secondly, publications like the *Journal* of the Kilkenny Society, the *Ulster Journal of Archæology*, that of the Irish Archæological Society, the *Proceedings* and other works emanating from the Royal Irish Academy, amongst which the Catalogue of Antiquities preserved in the Museum of that body, by the late Sir William Wilde, takes a foremost place, were well calculated to place students—particularly of Celtic archæology—in the right way of investigation. But besides the Societies, not a few independent observers were individually at work.

It is scarcely necessary here to particularize the names of these generally successful searchers for antiquarian truths; suffice it to say that, one way or another, within the last forty years or so a flood of new light has been thrown upon many subjects relating to Irish archæology, and that Ireland now confessedly stands the richest storehouse in Western Europe of Celtic monuments of, it may be said, every class known to the learned in such matters.

The "Handbook" to which reference has already been made, and of which the present volume may be considered a doubly-enlarged successor, has long been out of print, and for years has been unobtainable, except, indeed, when a copy might now and then turn up under the auctioneer's hammer at the dispersion of some library. In a degree it had become antiquated, though, as far as it went, it possessed the character, I believe, of being accurate and trustworthy. All the matter which it contained will be found in the present issue, together with a vast amount of new information, the result generally of personal observation on my own part of more than one class of monuments, the very existence of which was not known even to our most accomplished antiquaries forty years ago.

Not a few of the subjects upon which it is my province now to treat have, especially of late years, excited considerable attention not only in Ireland, but even in countries beyond the limits of the British Empire. Much has been already done, yet much remains to be accomplished. It is not sufficient to have shown that Ireland contains an unbroken series of monuments, many of them historical, which lead us back, step by step, to a period long anterior to the conversion of her people to Christianity,—to have formed museums,—to have translated annals and manuscripts relating to her history and antiquities;—a feeling should be awakened in the breasts of the people generally to preserve with scrupulous care the numerous remains of early Irish art with which the country everywhere abounds, and which frequently, in local history, form our only records. The anxiety which the various governments of Europe, even the most despotic, evince for the preservation and con-servation of their antiquities shows how widely their importance is recognized. It is even so, especially of late years, in America.

In the following pages I do not promise my readers any very wonderful discoveries, any startling facts. I am content to describe the various remains as they are to be found, prefixing to each chapter observations more or less elaborate, as the case may require, relative to the era, peculiarities, and probable or ascertained uses of the particular class of monument to which it is devoted. The volume, it is hoped, may be useful to the educated antiquary, as well as to the student— to the former as a guide, directing his attention to many remains of great interest of most easy access from the metropolis, and hitherto altogether unnoticed, or described in books of the existence of which he may have no knowledge, or of which he may not with ease be able to procure copies; to the latter, in like manner as a guide, and also as containing information not merely of the locality wherein studies may be found.

The book, I trust, may be largely read by Irishmen. There are few true natives of the soil who would not resent any charge of coldness or indifference to the welfare of their country, or of *wilful* ignorance upon the subject of her history or antiquities which might be urged against them. Yet most of our travelled countrymen are better acquainted with the appearance of the Rhine than with that of the Shannon; with the windings of the Thames than with those of the Boyne; their knowledge of these glorious Irish rivers being probably just so much as may be acquired from

a school geography, while they have explored the
reaches of the Thames, and elaborately *"done"* the
chief points upon the Rhine. Yet there is no country
in Europe where a stranger, even the proverbial "un-
protected female," may so safely travel as in Ireland.
When in his work, entitled "Rude Stone Monuments
of all Countries," James Fergusson, D.C.L., F.R.S.,
&c. &c., treats of the antiquities of Carrowmore, near
Sligo (a locality described by Petrie as, with the
exception of Carnac, in Brittany, containing the
largest assemblage of cromleacs and other megalithic
monuments hitherto discovered in the world), he
appends the following note :—

"Carrowmore is more easily accessible than Carnac. The inns
at Sligo are better than those of Auray, the remains are within
three miles of the town, and the scenery near Sligo is far more
beautiful than that of the Morbihan; yet hundreds of our
countrymen rush annually to the French megaliths, and bring
home sketch-books full of views and measurements, but no one
thinks of the Irish monuments, and no views of them exist that
are in any way accessible to the public."

The stones of the great carns on Slieve-na-Calliagh,
or the Hag's Mountain, near Oldcastle, Co. Meath,
and those of Dowth and Newgrange in the same
county, together, exhibit a greater number of archaic
carvings (circles, spirals, cups, dots, &c. &c.) than are

to be found in Britain, Caledonia, and Gaul united !
Yet hardly a score of visitors seek them in a year,
though they may be reached from Dublin in little
more than two hours.

To the Council of the Royal Irish Academy, and
to the Committee of the Royal Society of Antiquaries
of Ireland, I am indebted for permission to reproduce in the following pages a number of beautiful
woodcuts which originally appeared in their respective
publications.

The subjects, with very few exceptions, were drawn
and transferred to the blocks by myself; and it is
only fair to add that Mr. George Hanlon and Messrs.
Oldham have, in the execution of these cuts, proved
themselves admirable artists as engravers on wood.

CONTENTS.

PART I.

𝔓𝔞𝔤𝔞𝔫 𝔄𝔫𝔱𝔦𝔮𝔲𝔦𝔱𝔦𝔢𝔰.

CHAPTER I.

PILLAR STONES, AND OTHER RUDE MONUMENTS.

CHAPTER II.

CHAPTER III.

PRIMITIVE FUNERAL RITES.

CHAPTER IV.

GRAVES AND CEMETERIES.

CHAPTER V.

STONE CIRCLES AND ALIGNMENTS.

CHAPTER VI.

RATHS AND DUNS—THE LIS OR CATHAIR—THE CASHEL— SUBTERRANEAN CHAMBERS.

PART II.
Early Christian Antiquities.

CHAPTER I.

ORATORIES.

CHAPTER II.

CHURCHES.

CHAPTER III.

EARLY DECORATED CHURCHES.

CHAPTER IV.

CROSSES, ETC.

CHAPTER V.

ROUND TOWERS.

PART III.

Anglo-Irish Remains.

CHAPTER I.

ABBEYS, ETC.

CHAPTER II.

FONTS.

CHAPTER III.

CASTLES.

CHAPTER IV.

TOWN GATES, GATE TOWERS, AND WALLS.

PART IV.
Miscellaneous Notices.

—

CHAPTER I.

BRIDGES AND CAUSEWAYS.

CHAPTER II.

THE "CRANNOG," OR LAKE HABITATION, AS FOUND IN IRELAND.

CHAPTER III.

MISCELLANEOUS FINDS—ECCLESIASTICAL FURNITURE, ETC.

CHAPTER IV.

ECCLESIASTICAL REMAINS IN THE COLLECTION OF THE ROYAL IRISH ACADEMY.

LIST OF ILLUSTRATIONS.

ARCHÆOLOGIA HIBERNICA.

INTRODUCTION.

N Archæological Student, upon arriving in Dublin, the metropolis of a country more remarkable, perhaps, than any other of the West of Europe for the number, the variety, and, it may be said, the *nationality* of its ancient remains, seeks in vain for a Handbook containing the kind of information he peculiarly requires. He is referred, indeed, by the "guides" to our two Cathedrals, the Castle, and perhaps one or two other structures in the city, or its immediate vicinity, for the exercise of his favourite study. In the subjects alluded to he finds only tolerable examples of a style of architecture which is by no means characteristic of Irish mediæval remains, and which appears never in this country to have attained the same degree of magnificence for which in England, and elsewhere, it is so remarkable. At the same time we have, within easy access from Dublin, representatives, many of them in a fine state of preservation, of almost every structure of antiquarian

interest to be met with in any part of the kingdom.
Sepulchral tumuli—several of which, in point of rude
magnificence, are, confessedly, unrivalled in Europe—
stone circles, cromleacs, pillar-stones,

> "The carns' gray pyramid
> Where urns of mighty chiefs lie hid,"

and other remains of the earliest period of society in Ireland, lie within a journey of less than two hours from
the metropolis. The cromleacs of Howth, Kilternan,
Shanganagh, Mount Venus, Hollypark, Shankill,
and of the Druid's Glen, near Cabinteely, may be
reached almost in a morning's walk from Dublin; and
a journey of seventy minutes from the Amiens-street
Terminus of the Great Northern Railway, with a car
drive of about four miles, will give the student of Irish
antiquities an opportunity of viewing at Monasterboice,
near Drogheda, amongst other remains, two crosses, the
most grand and beautiful, not only in this country, but
perhaps in Christendom.

So numerous are the monuments of a period, even
antecedent to the first recorded Scandinavian invasion
of Ireland, lying within a few hours' journey from
Dublin, that it would be tedious and unnecessary to
notice them all; a judicious selection will answer every
purpose of the inquirer.

In order to make the subject more clearly understood I shall classify the various remains under three
heads:—1. Pagan, embracing those which upon the
best authority are presumed to have existed previous

to, or within a limited period after the general introduction of Christianity, in the fifth century; II. The Early Christian, including the Round Towers, &c. &c.; and III. The Anglo-Irish.

Under the head of Anglo-Irish shall be found notices of such structures as were erected during days recently subsequent to the English invasion, and which, though often of Irish foundation, appear generally to have been built upon Anglo-Norman, or English models.

The remains which may be considered of the Pagan era consist of cromleacs, carns, stone circles, pillar-stones, tumuli, duns, raths, forts, rock markings, &c. They are found in considerable numbers particularly in the more remote parts of the kingdom, where, from the thinness of the population, and the absence of any modern "*improvement,*" they have been suffered to remain unmolested, save by the hand of time.

The very immediate neighbourhood of Dublin, for obvious reasons, is less rich in antiquities of this primitive class than in that of the others; but the railways afford ready access to several most interesting monuments.

Of relics of early Christian architecture we have numerous examples, no fewer than five Round Towers lying within a short distance of the city.

Of the early churches of Ireland—structures of a period when the "Scotish (Irish) monkes in Ireland and Britaine highly excelled in their holinesse and learning, *yea sent forth whole flockes of most devout men into all parts of Europe*" (see Camden's *Hibernia*, p. 67)—

there are specimens in a state of preservation sufficient
to give a good idea of architecture, in what may be
considered its second stage in Ireland. The peculiarities of a more advanced style will be found noticed.

The remains referred to under the head of Anglo-
Irish consist of castles, abbeys, town-gates, &c. &c.
The great lords who, in the time of Henry the Second,
or of his immediate successors, received grants of land
from the Crown would necessarily erect fortresses of
considerable strength and extent, the more securely to
preserve their possessions from the inroads of the native
Irish, with whom they were usually at war. The castles
of Trim, Malahide, Howth, Carlow, and a host of others,
are silent witnesses to the fact that the early invaders
were occasionally obliged to place some faith in the
efficacy of strong walls and towers, to resist the ad-
vances of their restless neighbours, who for several
centuries subsequent to the invasion were rather the
levellers than the builders of castles. Of the massive
square keep, so common in every part of the kingdom,
our neighbourhood furnishes several examples. As,
except in some minor details, they usually bear a great
resemblance to each other, an inspection of one or two
will afford a just idea of all. They were generally used
as the residence of a chieftain, or as an outpost de-
pendent upon some larger fortress in the neighbourhood.
Many appear to have been erected by English settlers,
and they are usually furnished with a bawn, or enclosure, into which cattle were driven at night, a precaution very significant of the times. Our abbeys, though

frequently of considerable extent and magnificence, are in general more remarkable for the simple grandeur of their proportions. The finest exhibit many characteristics of what in England is called the "transition style"; but early pointed is also found, and in great purity. There are in Ireland but few very notable examples of the succeeding styles. Decoration, indeed, was not so great a *desideratum* as strength and security; and we do not want the evidence of annals to show that our abbeys had occasionally to stand upon their defence, as bartizans surmount the doorways of several.

Having now introduced my readers to the subject generally, it only remains to be added that under the heading *Miscellaneous Notices* a description will be found of certain antiquities which it seemed impossible to class with the monuments referred to in the three preceding headings. Many of our lake dwellings, or crannogs, for instance, are believed, with good reason, by antiquarians of note, to have been in use even in pagan times in Ireland; several of these islets, however, are recorded to have been occupied as places of human habitation so late as the seventeenth century. It would, therefore, be hazardous to classify them with either pagan or Christian remains, and it is certain that they are not Anglo-Irish. For ready reasons the torques and golden ornaments, weapons, &c. &c., are described under the "Miscellaneous" heading; and though the bells, crosses, and reliquaries are obviously of a Christian period, it seemed advisable that they should be noticed in company with the other objects of metal.

In the following pages I propose to give a carefully executed illustration of several of the more remarkable specimens of each class of remains described, pointing out their various characteristics, and in every case referring the reader to the original.

The greatest degree of care has been exercised in order to give faithful representations. With very few exceptions, the original sketches have been made upon the spot, and transferred to wood by the writer. It may be stated that until the appearance of the former "Handbook" the greater portion of the subjects which it contained had never been previously published.

PART I.
Pagan Antiquities.

CHAPTER I.

PILLAR STONES, AND OTHER RUDE MONUMENTS.

THEIR VARIETY—THE SPEAKING STONES NEAR OLDCASTLE—THE LIA
FAIL AT TARA—OTHER EXAMPLES—HOLED STONES—ROCK SCRIBINGS
AND CUP MARKINGS—DRUIDS' CHAIRS OR SEATS—BULLAN STONES.

ILLAR STONES are found in many parts of
Ireland, and particularly in districts
where stone circles, carns, and cromleacs occur. They are usually rough
monoliths, and evidently owe their upright position, not to accident, but to
the design and labour of an ancient people. They are
usually called by the native Irish, *Gallauns* or *Leaghauns*,
and in character they are precisely similar to the Hoar-
stones of England, the Hare-stane of Scotland, the
Maen-qwyr of Wales; and the Continental *Menhir*.

Many theories have been promulgated relative to
their origin. They are supposed to have been idol-

stones, to have been erected as landmarks, &c., and
lastly, to have been monumental stones recording the
scene of a battle, or the spot upon which a warrior
had fallen. The name "*cat-stone*," by which some
examples are known in Scotland, would well warrant
such an idea, the word *cath* in the Gaelic language
signifying a battle. There is indeed a strong probability that not a few of these mysterious waifs
of time found in Ireland were raised in honour of
long departed chieftains, who had met their fate on
or near the spot whereon the stone stands; others
may have marked boundaries, or have been used
as idols. At either end of the famous historic
ford over the river Erne, at Ballyshannon, may
be seen two remarkable examples—to that on the
northern side other stones would seem to lead.
This is a very significant fact in favour of the land-
mark theory. At the same time we learn from the
history of St. Patrick's labours in still pagan Erin
that he found the people worshipping certain idols
in the form of stone pillars, some of which he caused
to be overthrown, while upon one purposely left
standing he inscribed the name of Jesus. There can
be little question that the saint and his immediate
followers, in their horror of all that was idolatrous,
destroyed a large number of the pillar-stones which,
"time out of mind," had been venerated, or even
worshipped by our heathenish ancestors; but, nevertheless, a considerable number appear to have been
allowed to remain. These, in not a few instances,

would seem to have been consecrated to the Faith, and from having been idols were transformed into memorials of the triumph of Christianity. We are not without satisfactory evidence of such adaptation having been effected. Several of our apparently oldest lithic monuments may be observed rudely punched, not carved, with the figure of a primitive cross, accompanied by one or other of the inscriptions Dni, Dno, or Dom. Probably, if carefully looked for in sequestered localities, many other examples might be found, particularly in the islands off the southern and western coasts. Dr. Todd, in his *Life of St. Patrick*, has, I believe, conclusively shown that the generally received idea of the sudden, and, it may be said, miraculous conversion of Ireland in the days of the saint, and in those of his immediate successors, to be wholly erroneous.

In several parts of the country the gallaun is still considered by many of the people to be something weird, and, " to be let alone."

"About two miles north-west of Oldcastle," wrote the late E. A. Conwell, in his book on the supposed tomb of Ollaṁh ꝼoṽhla, there is a townland called *Fearan-na-gloch* (from ꝼeaꝑan, land, and cloċ, a stone), so called from two remarkable stone flags, still to be seen standing in it, popularly called clocha labaꝑċha, *i. e.* "the speaking stones": and these stones also give a local name to the green pasture-field in which they are situated, which is called paiꝑc naʒ-clocha-labaꝑċha, *i. e.* " field of the speaking stones."

"There can be little doubt," he proceeds, "the pagan rites of incantation and divination had been practised at these stones, as their very name, so curiously handed down to us, imports; for, in the traditions of the neighbourhood, it is even yet current that they have been consulted in cases where either man or beast was supposed to have been ' *overlooked*'; that they were infallibly effective in curing the consequences of the ' evil eye'; and that they were deemed to be unerring in naming the individual through whom these evil consequences came. Even up to a period not very remote, when anything happened to be lost or stolen, these stones were invariably consulted; and in cases where cattle, &c., &c., had strayed away, the directions they gave for finding them were considered as certain to lead to the desired result. There was one peremptory inhibition, however, to be scrupulously observed in consulting these stones, viz. that they were *never* to be asked to give the same information a second time, as they, under no circumstances whatever, would repeat an answer." These conditions having, about seventy or eighty years ago, been violated by an ignorant inquirer who came from a distance, the " speaking stones" became dumb, and have so remained ever since. Two of these relics (there were originally four) of a long, long past are at present extant. The larger may be described as consisting of a thin slab of laminated sandy grit. Its dimensions are as follows :—Total height above ground, as nearly as possible, 7 feet ; extreme breadth, 5 feet

8 inches; breadth near summit, 3 feet 6 inches; average thickness, about 8 inches. In no part does it exhibit the mark of a chisel or hammer. The height of the second remaining stone, above the present level of the ground, is 6 feet 4 inches, or thereabouts; it is in breadth, at base, 3 feet 4 inches, and near the top 1 foot more; thickness at base, 14 inches. The material, unlike that found in the generality of such monuments, is blue lime-stone.

Perhaps the most remark-able example of the pillar stone, as found in Ireland, occurs on the celebrated Hill of Tara, Co. Meath. This very mysterious monu-ment at present occupies a position in the centre of the *Forradh*, one of the principal

Pillar Stone at Tara, supposed to be the Lia Fail, or Stone of Destiny.

earthworks still remaining on that memorable site. The stone formerly stood upon, or rather by the side of, a small mound lying within the enclosure of *Rath Righ*, and called Dumha-na-n-Giall, or the Mound of the Hostages. In 1798 it was placed in its present posi-tion, to mark the grave of some men then recently slain in an encounter with the king's troops.

As suggested by Dr. Petrie it is extremely probable that this pillar, or *Menhir*, is no other than the cele-brated Lia Fail, or Stone of Destiny, upon which during many ages the monarchs of Ireland were crowned, and which is generally supposed to have been removed from Ireland to Scotland for the coronation of Fergus Mac Earck, a prince of the blood-royal of Ireland, there having been a prophecy that in whatever country this famous stone was preserved, a king of the Scotic race should reign.

Certain it is that in the mss. to which Dr. Petrie refers (one of which is probably of the tenth century of our era), the stone is mentioned as still existing at Tara ; and, " it is," writes the doctor, " an interesting fact, that a large obeliscal pillar stone, in a prostrate position, occupied till a recent period the very situation on the hill pointed out as the place of the Lia Fail, by the Irish writers of the tenth, eleventh, and twelfth centuries." Dr. Petrie, after remarking upon the want of agreement between the Irish and Scottish accounts of the history of the Lia Fail, and on the questionable character of the evidence upon which the story of its removal from Ireland rests, observes : " That it is in the highest degree improbable, that, to gratify the desire of a colony, the Irish would have voluntarily parted with a monument so venerable for its antiquity, and deemed essential to the legitimate succession of their own kings."

If the Irish authorities for the existence of the Lia Fail at Tara, so late as the tenth, eleventh, or twelfth century, may be relied upon, and their extreme accuracy in other respects is sufficiently clear, the stone carried away from Scotland by Edward the First, and

now preserved in Westminster Abbey, under the coronation chair, has long attracted a degree of celebrity
to which it was not entitled, while the veritable Lia
Fail, the stone which, according to the early bardic
accounts, *roared* beneath the ancient Irish monarchs at
their inauguration, remained forgotten and disregarded
among the green raths of deserted Tara.

At Clogher, Co. Tyrone, a very curious stone has for
ages been preserved. It is thus noticed by Harris, in
his edition of Ware's Bishops :—" Clogher, situated on
the river Lanny, takes its name from a golden stone,
from which in the times of paganism The Devil used
to pronounce Juggling Answers, like the Oracles of
Apollo Pythius." Harris, however, was incorrect in
his statement that the city derived its name from this
idol; there are many other places in Ireland similarly
called, where no pillar or other remarkable stone can
be pointed to.

Some of our finest and perhaps oldest pillar stones
bear cup and circle markings, similar to those found
upon the face of undisturbed rocks in various parts of
Ireland, Britain, the European Continent, and even of
America. A very remarkable example, which occurs
at Muff, about five miles from Londonderry, has been
described in the Journal of the Royal Historical and
Archæological Association, by the late Rev. James
Graves, who states that the stone, which stood about
8 feet in height, and measured 4 feet 6 inches across
at the base, by 2 feet 6 inches in thickness, was on one
of its faces covered with cup and circle sculpturings,

some of which exhibited the central channels which appear on the rock sculptures in Kerry. The meaning of these channels no antiquary has yet ascertained. " Where the soil had covered the base, two of the cups, with their concentric circles, were very plain and unworn ; but the water trickling from a hollow on the top of the stone, had injured some of those above. Excavations were made to a depth of four feet round the base of the *Menhir ;* but no trace of interment, or relic of any kind, was discovered." He states, however, " close to the stone was found a kind of bone earth, or soil mixed with minute fragments of bone, apparently not human, but from their minute and decomposed state identification was impossible."

G. H. Kinahan, in pages of the Journal already referred to, figures and describes a most remarkable *Menhir* which he found in Donegal. In this instance four of the cups are so arranged that the channels extending from them form a perfect cross of the Roman character. Here the likeness to the Christian symbol cannot be considered other than accidental. A device, almost precisely similar, is found upon a rude stone monument in Scotland ; and we know that upon the bases of not a few of the cinerary urns, formed of baked clay, discovered in cists in Ireland, and found to contain calcined human bones, flint arrow heads, bone implements, &c. &c., a cruciform ornament may not unfrequently be noticed. This, at least as so placed, cannot be considered a Christian symbol.

Several of our pillar stones, yet *in situ,* and a great

many others overthrown, or removed, present Ogam inscriptions. Immediately near Kesh, a station on the railway line between Enniskillen and Bundoran, occur a carn, an earthen sepulchral mound, and a *Menhir* of enormous proportions. The latter, upon its south-western angle, bore a legend in Ogam characters, which some years ago, when a *savant* from the south was expected to come and examine it, was, by a man named Gerard Irvine (whose intentions were no doubt praiseworthy) so scraped, cleaned, and "improved," that little trace of the original remains. The subject of Ogam writing or scoring will be found touched on in a subsequent chapter. In the meantime I give an illustration of portion of a pillar stone, bearing a well-marked legend in Ogam letters. The original, which may be seen in the Library of Trinity College, Dublin, formerly stood in the county of Kerry.

Ogam Stone in Trinity College, Dublin.

Of the ordinary plain Gallaun, pillar stone, or *Menhir*, the annexed illustration, representing one of several remaining in the vicinity of the tumulus of Newgrange (hereafter to be noticed), will afford a good idea. It measures 9 feet in height, and in cir-cumference 16. A similar monolith, in the village of

Ballynacraig (*i. e.* Rock Town) to which it probably gave its name, about half a mile from Newgrange,

measures 24 feet in girth, but its present height above ground is only about 6 feet. There are monuments of a similar class in the valley of Glenismole—the glen of the thrush — beyond Rathfarnham, about five and a half miles or so from Dublin.

Strange to say some of these remains, whether monuments, boundary stones, or idols, appear to have been known by particular names, as, for instance, a grand specimen, standing, amongst a group of megalithic structures, in the sandhills of Finner, a wild district extending between Ballyshannon and Bundoran. It is called " *Fleatuch* "; what that appellation means I have utterly failed to ascertain, nor was more successful in a search after the significance of " *Eglone,*" the name by which a boulder, rising 18 feet in height, and measuring on two sides 7 feet 6 inches, and 11 feet 6 inches on the others, is known amongst the peasantry of Moytirra, Co. Sligo. This enormous monolith stands perfectly upright, is rudely symmetrical in form, and has the appearance of a Gallaun or *Menhir.* It is in all probability by the agency of ice that this mass of grey magnesian limestone was torn from its natural bed and placed

Standing Stone near
Newgrange.

as we now find it. No legendary tale concerning the "Eglone" at present remains, but the stone, or rather rock, is regarded by not a few of the neighbouring people as possessed of mysterious attributes, of some kind or other, which they cannot explain: it was in all probability an idol.

At a place called Keimaneigh, in the southern part of the county of Cork, standing in the immediate vicinity of some very primitive remains, is a true pillar stone, which is supposed by natives of the locality to represent a woman who for her numerous sins, and scorn of repentance, had been thus petrified. The pillar, which is about 6 feet high, bears a rude resemblance to a female human figure ; hence, no doubt, the origin of the legend.

Of the hundreds of pillar stones remaining in Ireland the great majority unquestionably belong to periods with us usually styled pre-historic. The date of one example, however, of ante-Patrician time has been satisfactorily settled. Cruachan, or Rathcrogan, situated about five miles from Carrick-on-Shannon, consists of a *mur*, circular in form, and composed of stone. "Within this," writes Petrie, "are small circular mounds, which, when examined, are found to cover rude sepulchral chambers, formed of stone, without cement of any kind, and containing unburnt bones." Outside the rath, or enclosure, in the centre of a small tumulus, is a pillar, referred to in the following notice of it by Duald Mac Firbis : "The body of Dathi was brought to Cruachan, and was

interred at Relig-na-Riogh, where most of the kings
of the race of Heremon were buried, and where to this
date the red stone pillar remains on a stone monument
over his grave, near Rath Cruachan, to this time
(1666)." Dathi was the last pagan monarch of
Ireland. He died in the beginning of the fifth century from the effects of lightning while leading his
army on a continental raid. The scene of his death
was in the neighbourhood of the Alps.

Holed Stones.—Perforated stones, very similar to
the ordinary pillar stone, are found in many parts of
Ireland, Scotland, and even, as appears from Mr.
Wilford's Asiatic Researches, in India. Abroad, as
well as at home, their origin is shrouded in the deepest
mystery, and it is not likely that the subject can ever
be fully elucidated.

In Ireland they are generally associated with pre-
historic remains, and are occasionally found in connexion with our earliest, and only earliest, ecclesiastical
establishments. As has been already suggested what
they were primarily intended for, no man can say. It
is highly probable that they had their origin in days
most remote, and that, somehow or other, perhaps like
the "holy wells," they became, as it were, pressed into
association with Christian rites.

Mr. Wilford, in his work already pointed out (vol. vi.,
p. 502), states that perforated stones are not uncommon
in India, and devout people pass through them when the
opening will admit, in order to be *regenerated*. If the

hole be too small, they put the hand or foot through it, and with a sufficient degree of faith it answers nearly the same purpose.

I do not now profess to give a list of holed stones to be found in connexion with our old churches, but I have noticed examples in Castledermot, Co. Kildare; Kilmalkedar, Co. Kerry; Inismurray, Co. Sligo; Killbarry, near Tarmon Barry, on the Shannon; Mainister, on Aran Mòr, Co. Galway; and on the Island of Devenish in Lough Erne, Co. Fermanagh. Many other instances might be adduced.

We have perhaps lived beyond the age when legends referring to this class of monument were still generally current. The virtue of the Kilmalkedar stone was some thirty or forty years ago equal in repute to that conceded to the Stennis example, and even, in some respects, superior; for, it was further firmly believed by many of the old inhabitants of Kerry, that persons afflicted with chronic rheumatism, "falling sickness," or some other ills, might, by passing three times round it (with faith, and by the offering of certain prayers), be restored to health. For many years past, however, owing to the influence of the clergy of all denominations, and the spread of education among the masses, the reverence once awarded to such relics has lost its superstitious element, though respect for the work of the ancient people is often happily preserved.

Concerning the celebrated holed stone of Stennis, Mr. Fergusson, in his work on the "Rude Stone Monuments of All Countries," seems to have held very

peculiar ideas. With these I have at present nothing
to do; but when he states that there is no proof of a
holed stone being used in any Celtic cemetery for purposes similar to those practised at the Stennis example,
he only commits one of the hundred, and more, mis-
takes made by him, and heedlessly published in his
dissertation on Irish antiquities. Unquestionably not
a few of our holed stones are of doubtful character,
inasmuch as they may be classified either as, with us,
pre-historic, or belonging to an early period of Christianity. It is impossible to look upon what probably constitutes the finest monument of this class, remaining in
Ireland, without assigning to it a degree of antiquity
equal at least to that acknowledged to be possessed by
the cromleacs, circles, and other megoliths of Carrowmore, immediately adjoining. Of this stone Colonel
Wood-Martin, in his learned and deeply interesting
work, entitled " Rude Stone Monuments in Sligo,"
gives the following original notice and description :—
" It marks the point of junction of the three parishes
of the district formerly, and still by the country people,
designated *Cuil-irra*. This boundary mark is a thin
limestone flag, set on edge; it is 9 feet in height and
10 feet in breadth above ground. The little stream
which issues from Tobernavean, or *Tobar-na-bh Fian*,
the ' Well of the Warriors,' laves its base, which must
be deeply buried in the earth. Toward the east side
this flag-stone is pierced by a squarish, or rather an
oblong, perforation, 3 feet in length by 2 feet in
breadth. From its mottled appearance this slab is

popularly called *Cloch-bhreac*, or the 'Speckled Stone';
also *Cloch-lia*, or the 'Gray Stone.'" Another pre-
sumedly pagan example, standing upwards of five feet
in height above the present neighbouring level of the
ground, may be seen upon an eminence in the im-

Holed Stone in Cuil-irra, Co. Sligo.

mediate vicinity of Doagh, a village in the county of
Antrim. In the same district, near Cushendall, a
second fine holed stone until lately existed. Probably
one of the most curious monuments of the class under

notice, remaining in Ireland, formerly stood in the very ancient Christian cemetery of Inniskeen (close to the *Cloictheach*, or round tower belfry), Co. Monaghan. It is now prostrate. This relic, which is composed of porphyry, has an aperture through it sufficiently large to admit the insertion of a goodly-sized human arm. Not very long ago it was the custom at Easter to fix in the perforation a pole, up which for a prize the neighbouring young people used to climb. The stone is said to have been formerly used for superstitious purposes, but unfortunately no particulars of the rites or customs then practised are now recollected.

The most famous holed stone in the world is doubtlessly that of Stennis, near Kirkwall in Orkney, already referred to. It has been immortalized in his tale of "The Pirate" by Sir Walter Scott. As stated by Fergusson in his notice of Stennis, "it is quite certain that the oath of Woden, or Odin, was sworn by persons joining their hands through the hole in this ring stone, and that an oath so taken, although by Christians, was deemed solemn and binding." This ceremony was held so very sacred that anyone breaking it was accounted infamous and a person to be shunned.

In his "Journey to the Orkney Islands," in 1781, Principal Gordon gives the following anecdote :— "The young man was called before the session, and the elders were particularly severe. Being asked by the minister the cause of so much severity, they answered, 'You do not know what a bad man this is; he has broken the promise of Odin,' and further explained that the contracting parties had joined hands through the hole in the stone."

All this, no doubt, may be very interesting to lovers of folk lore ; but in what manner does the anecdote serve to indicate the original character of the Stennis monument ? That it was at one time sacred to Odin, or Woden, and no doubt reverenced by pagan northmen and their successors, perhaps for many generations, is little to the point. We are told that even Christians used the stone on certain solemn occasions. Why may not the Scandinavian occupiers of Orkney have, as it were, adopted a pillar which they found associated with old world customs and memories, and dedicated it to Woden, or Odin, or indeed to any other member of their Valhalla ?

Few who have paid even passing attention to the subject of Irish antiquities, recognising the fact that several of our holed stones, bearing apertures of considerable size, and found in the immediate neighbourhood of remains universally acknowledged to belong to days of paganism, will assume, I think, that the former do not partake of the same primeval character as the stone circles, carns, &c. &c., referred to.

But in Ireland we find at least two classes of perforated monoliths—the one I believe to be pre-historic ; the other to be, possibly, of ante-Christian times in Ireland, and to have been consecrated to the religious services of a people recently won to Christianity, but who still possessed some lingering reverence to the idols of their forefathers.

From my Paper on Inismurray, published in the Journal of the Royal Historical and Archæological Association of Ireland, for October, 1885, No. 64, the following notice of what may be considered the probably later class of holed stones is borrowed, in a slightly curtailed form:—

Inismurray presents three fine specimens of the pillar, two of which must be considered valuable and most rare examples of the " holed" class. For reasons presently to be explained these are sometimes called *Praying Stones* by the natives of the island. The more important stands on the southern side of *Teampull-na-Bfear*, or the " Church of the Men," at a little distance from that structure. It measures 4 feet in height, 11½ inches in breadth at top, 1 foot 1 inch at base, and about 7 inches in thickness. A graceful cross has been incised upon the front, or western side. It may be observed that the arms and head of the symbol terminate in spirals like those found upon the celebrated alphabet stone at Kilmalkedar, the work upon which has been held, by our best authorities on such matters, to belong to the sixth, or at latest to the seventh century of the Christian era. The monument faces east and west ; its edges and eastern side are plain. The western face exhibits two holes of a size just large enough to admit the insertion of a fairly-developed thumb. These orifices extend through the adjoining angles of the stone, and open out at its sides in apertures sufficiently spacious to receive the fingers of a hand of ordinary proportions. In connexion with this pillar, as also with a similar monument situated close to *Teampull-na-mban*, or " Church of the Women," a custom which is worthy of record, very generally prevails. Women who expect shortly to become mothers are wont to resort to these stones, for the purpose of praying for a happy issue from the perils of their impending travail. The natives assert that death in childbirth is an unknown calamity upon the island. The postulants kneel, passing their thumbs into the front, and their fingers into the side openings, by which means a firm grasp of the angles of the pillar is obtained. They are thus enabled to rise from their act of obeisance with a minimum of strain or difficulty.

A pillar stone, unperforated and uninscribed, of about the same dimensions as that just noticed, is seen immediately beside it. The two stand in line at right angles with the northern wall of the very ancient church, almost immediately adjoining.

The second holed stone, to which I have already referred, bears upon its eastern face a plain Latin cross. It is 5 feet high, $10\frac{1}{2}$ inches broad at base, $11\frac{1}{2}$ inches at top, and $4\frac{1}{2}$ inches in thickness. Like its fellow at the " Church of the Men" it is held in profound veneration, especially by the women of the island. The cross which it exhibits is characteristic of the earliest Christian times in Ireland ; this being so, the monument in its present style may be assigned to a period not later than the close of the sixth century. The pillar may indeed be pre-historic, and the cross an addition. It is much to be regretted that the Inismurray examples do not present lettering of any description. They are just of the kind upon which one might hope to find an inscription carved or punched in the Ogam character.

Rock Markings, Scorings, &c.—At the present day one subject of considerable interest, I may say to the archæologists of all civilized communities, remains to be solved. I allude to the so-called Rock Markings, or "Scribings," which, whether noticed upon European, Asiatic, or American rocks or monuments, often in their general features bear so strong a family likeness one to the other that it is at first sight difficult to believe that they had not been executed by one and the same race of people. Such an idea, however, it would be the essence of absurdity to entertain. Philosophers tell us that savages, or semi-savages, situated widely apart, and placed under somewhat similar climatic conditions, will instinctively run in parallel grooves of thought; and thus, in the form, material, and ornamentation of their objects of veneration, arms, and implements of everyday life, as well as in their personal decorations, present a like development. So also with their *Fetichism*, or religion, or by what other name the devotional feeling inherent in the hearts of even the most abject tribes may be styled. It need be no wonder then that, far and near, over the surface of the "Old" and of the "New World," rock and stone scribings, often of an unknown period, are to be found; and that they should frequently have much in common.

Yet how recently have archæologists noticed these

intensely mysterious antiquarian puzzles. Petrie does not seem to have heard of their existence; O'Donovan and O'Curry make no mention of them; nor do the older writers, except in one or two instances, where a single stone or so is referred to as bearing work of a mystic and barbarous character.

The Right Rev. Charles Graves (now Bishop of Limerick), in the "Transactions" of the Royal Irish Academy, appears to have been the first to draw attention to sculpturings of this class as occurring in Ireland, and to Irish examples, only, I shall now refer. Subsequently the subject was taken up by inquirers, in various parts of the world, who found in their own territories or districts kindred rock carvings. As yet no man can say what they were intended to represent, and until very many more than we know of at present shall have been examined and classified, it will be well to drop speculation concerning them. In the meantime it may be observed that the groups of designs found upon the surface of our undisturbed rocks exhibit in many instances characteristics almost, if not entirely, peculiar to themselves. For instance, the incomplete concentric circles with a central cup, from which extends a straight or slightly curved stroke, called "the channel," through, and sometimes beyond the outermost gap in the curved lines, are never observed amongst the almost infinite variety of figurings presented in our great sepulchral chambers. Again, the spirals of the stone sepulchres are, as far as I am aware, invariably absent in the array of designs found upon the undisturbed or natural rock. This circumstance was not left unobserved by Bishop Graves when describing his discoveries in Kerry. True it is that upon one small stone in the neighbourhood of Tulla-keel, near Sneem, he found a rude carving of a short portion of a spiral. This stone lay set in a fence; it may have belonged to some tomb of which no other relic is known to remain, so that little argument can be based on the character of its scribing.

As already intimated, although antiquaries are not yet in a position to pronounce authoritatively on the precise significance of our rock markings, a glance at some early speculations as to their nature may not be here out of place.

" It was to be presumed," wrote the Bishop, " that the persons who carved the inscriptions intended to represent circular objects of some kind or other. But what could these objects have been ? Some have suggested shields. This notion seems inconsistent with the fact that the same stone presents so many circular symbols of different sizes, varying from the small shallow cup of an inch or two in diameter to the group of concentric circles two feet across. It also seems probable that, as shields in general used to bear distinctive devices, these would appear in the inscriptions; but the inscribed circles exhibit no such variety as might have been expected on this hypothesis. Again, if the circles represented shields, what could be meant by the openings in the circumference of so many of them ? Lastly, what connexion could there be between the idea of shields and the long lines appearing in the Stague monument, or the short ones on that of Ballynasare?

"Another idea was that these figures were designed to represent astronomical phenomena."

For several reasons the learned writer could not accept that theory, particularly as it failed to account for the openings in the circles, and the accompanying lines.

" The idea which occurred to my own mind," he states, " was, that the incised circles were intended to represent the circular buildings of earth or stone, of which the traces still exist in every part of Ireland. This conjecture is supported by the following considerations :—

" 1. The circles are of different sizes, and some are disposed in concentric groups. The ancient dwellings and fortified seats of the ancient Irish were circular ; they were of various sizes, from the small cloghan, or stone house of ten feet in diameter, to the great camp including an area of some acres ; and the principal forts had several concentric *valla.*

" 2. The openings in the inscribed circles may have been intended to denote the entrances.

" 3. The other inscribed lines may have represented roads passing by or leading up to the forts.

" The conjecture that these carvings were primitive maps, representing the disposition of neighbouring forts, appeared to be a fanciful one ; and discouraged by the scepticism of friends to whom I communicated it, I laid aside the drawings and rubbings for some

years, hoping that some light might be thrown upon
the subject by the discovery of monuments the purpose
of which was evident.

"This expectation has not been fulfilled. Nevertheless I have some hope that my original guess has been
confirmed in such a way as to warrant me in submitting it for the judgment of our antiquaries.

"In the course of last autumn, after a careful examination of the drawings—those which had been made
chiefly of the Kerry examples—I came to the conclusion that the centres of the circles and the neighbouring cups and dots arrange themselves generally
three by three in straight lines. This disposition of
the symbols could not be said to be perfectly accurate ;
but I thought I could observe close and designed
approximation to it. If, then, the circles represent
forts, and are disposed three by three in straight lines
on the inscribed stones, I saw that we might expect to
find the forts disposed in like manner over the surface
of the country; and I think that I have succeeded in
verifying this inference. The ancient raths have fortunately been laid down on the six-inch Ordnance
Survey maps of Ireland; and unless I am deceived by
fortuitous collineations, I find that the forts are actually
arranged three by three in straight lines. The discovery of this fact, if it be a fact, would be of much
more consequence than the explanation of the meaning
of the inscriptions of which I have just given an
account. But this further inquiry must be conducted
with care. Large portions of the country must be ex-

amined, and those difficulties must be confronted which the disappearance of ancient remains must inevitably give rise to."

So the question of the meaning of a large majority of those primitive carvings seems, at least for the present, to stand.

It has been objected to the map theory that in the parts of Scotland and England where circle and channel scorings occur most numerously, no raths or forts, or if any, very few, are to be found. Upon this fact little stress need be laid, as the early British strongholds, corresponding to our raths, cathairs, duns, &c. &c., may, very frequently, in the manner of the sister island, have been composed of perishable materials, such as timber, or the interwoven branches of trees, stockades, in fact of which in the course of a few centuries, at most, no trace would remain.

The Bishop has hitherto published only a comparatively small portion of the rubbings and drawings which he was able to make, or procure, of the scorings under notice ; and it is certain that even in the districts examined by him very many have escaped observation. Mr. Robert Day, F.S.A., of Cork, has noticed and published some highly interesting examples which occur in his district ; the late G. V. Du Noyer mentions not a few which he found in various parts of the country ; other antiquarians have largely added to the list ; and chief amongst these is G. H. Kinahan, M.R.I.A., whose Papers in the Journal of the Royal Historical and Archæological Association, especially those descriptive

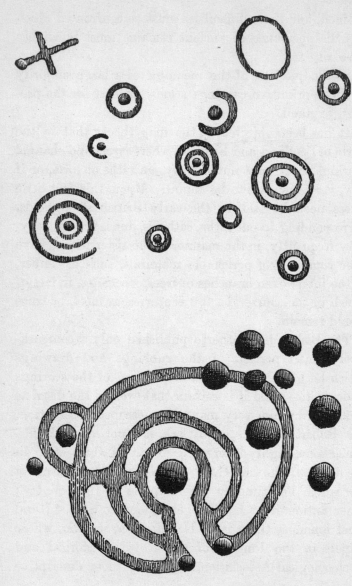

Rock Scribings, Co. Donegal, discovered by G. H. Kinahan, M.R.I.A. (Scale, one-fourth.)

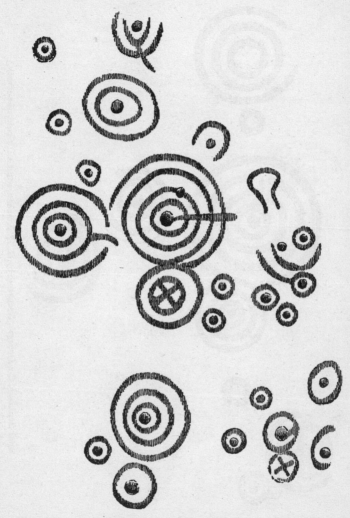

Rock Scribings, Co. Donegal, discovered by G. H. Kinahan, M.R.I.A.   (Scale, one-fourth.)

Rock Scribings, Co. Donegal, discovered by G. H. Kinahan, M.R.I.A. (Scale, one-fourth.)

of the Mevagh and Barnes inscriptions (Co. Donegal), have deservedly attracted great attention. Nevertheless Mr. Kinahan has not yet been able to give any account of a very great number of scorings which it was his lot to detect on certain undisturbed rocks scattered over the north-western district of Ireland, and lying chiefly in the Co. Donegal.

I myself was fortunate enough to discover, near Boho, Co. Fermanagh, about nine miles from Enniskillen, a cluster of large rocks bearing a vast number of the cup and circle devices. These subjects have all been engraved, and published in the pages of the Journal just referred to. In the same neighbourhood were similar markings on the living rock. They occur a little to the south of Lough Blocknet, on the slope of the hill. Many more might be here brought to light, were the scraw or skin of turf which covers the eminence removed.

It would thus appear that the scorings of the undisturbed rocks present only dots, cups, plain and entire, or imperfect concentric circles, and straight or curved lines.

In connexion with the sculpture found on the stones of sepulchral remains I shall have presently not a little to say. In the meantime it will be well to glance at a class of work which appears upon the walls of certain natural, or, perhaps, semi-artificial, caverns occurring at Knockmore, close to the village of Derrygonnelly, Co. Fermanagh. The chief of these is the " Lettered Cave," so called from the carvings, symbols, or inscrip-

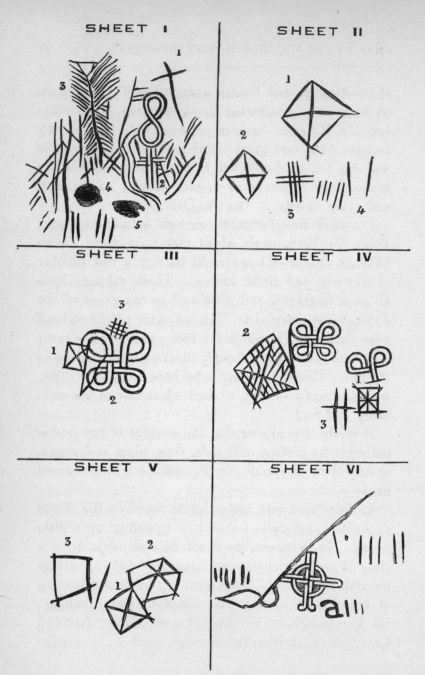

Scribings on sides of Knockmore Cave, near Derrygonnelly, Co. Fermanagh.
(Scale, one-third.)

tions of an early date with which its sides are scored. These are placed, without any attempt at symmetrical arrangement, upon almost every smooth portion of the rocky surface of the interior. Many are extremely well marked; others have become all but obliterated through the influence of time, the efflorescence of the stone, and the action of persons who have in many places scraped away the ancient figurings, or portions of them, in order to find space for the introduction of their respective obscure names, as visitors. Nevertheless a goodly portion of the ancient carving remains in a perfect condition, and in no place has it been completely destroyed. These scribings consist for the greater part of a number of figures and designs usually considered, by antiquaries, as pre-historic; others are clearly of an extremely early Christian date. The supposed older work consists of quadrangles, divided internally by lines extending from point to point (see sheets II., III., and V.), as also a leaf-shaped design like that found in monuments of a pagan, and, probably, archaic age in Ireland and in Brittany (see sheet I.). There are also numerous cups, knots, and dots, and many irregular lines which would suggest the idea of some ogamic kind of writing (see sheet II.). But whatever may be the age and character of such carvings, there can be no doubt amongst antiquaries that an elaborately-formed interlacing cross, which may be seen engraved upon the left-hand side of the entrance to the cave, must be referred to an early Christian period (see sheet VI.).

The first notice of these scribings appears to have been made by Mr. P. Magennis, a talented schoolmaster under the Board of National Education, residing at Knockmore, who sent some tracings, rubbings, or rough drawings of a small portion of the engravings to the late Rev. C. Reade, by whom they were forwarded to the late Rev. James Graves. That enthusiastic archæologist, with his characteristic zeal, laid the drawings, &c. &c., before Professor George Stephens, F.S.A. (a very high authority on the subject of Scandinavian inscriptions), who, in a letter addressed from Cheapinghaven, Denmark, described the work as representing "Scribbles of the Northmen, wild runes, and blind runes not now decipherable." Mr. Magennis, who kindly drew my attention to the cave, was very willing to acknowledge that his attempt to copy the markings was anything but satisfactory to himself. There are at any rate no scorings at present in the place from which the " diagram," from which Professor Stephens drew his deduction, could have been copied. The dimensions of this singular retreat are as follows :— Height, at the mouth, 10 feet 5 inches ; these proportions gradually lessen to a distance of about 18 feet from the external opening. There the passage takes an oblique turning to the southward, and continues to a distance of about 9 feet further into the heart of the limestone. The height of the chamber at its extreme end is about 5 feet. The opening faces north-east, and is well sheltered from the wind by a grassy knoll, which extends, right and left, in front.

The cave would be considered a dry, airy, and even luxuriant habitation, by persons accustomed to occupy the ordinary rath habitation as a place of retreat or repose. There is reason to believe that for many ages it was so utilized.

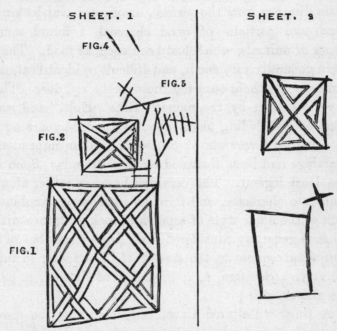

Scribings in Gillies' Hole, a Cave in Knockmore, Co. Fermanagh.
(Scale, one-third.)

Knockmore contains on its northern side, in a situation rather difficult of access, a second inscribed and partially artificial cavern.

This little eyry, which is only large enough to retain in a recumbent position two, or at least three, persons of ordinary size, must while yet the slopes of the knock

were covered with trees and brushwood, have formed a
very secure retreat. That it was inhabited in very
early days is certain, as upon digging up a considerable
portion of the floor, indications of fires having been used
were traceable on at least three separate levels. At a
little distance from the surface, amongst burnt-looking
earth and particles of wood charcoal, I found some
bones of animals, which had been used as food. They
were generally very small, and difficult of identification,
but amongst them occurred those of the red deer. The
cave is known by the name "Gillie's Hole," and was
used as an abiding place, about a hundred years ago,
by a pair of lovers who in consequence of an imprudent
marriage had been discarded by their friends. Such is
the local legend. The carvings here are rather of an
elaborate character, and form an interesting combina-
tion of the older style of sepulchral rock-sculpture with
what is generally considered early Irish work, but of a
period subsequent to the spread of Christianity in this
country. (See figs. 1, 2, 3, and 4 of sheet I., p. 39;
see also sheet II.)

A third "Lettered Cave," situated, "as the crow
flies," three-and-a-half miles from that of Knockmore,
and slightly over four from the police station of Boho,
contains some very interesting examples of cavern
scorings. There is no road or path by which it can be
approached nearer to it than four miles. No antiquary
or lover of nature whose fortune it may be to visit
Enniskillen, or the neighbourhood of Derrygonnelly,
should fail to visit this weird spot. A walk of four

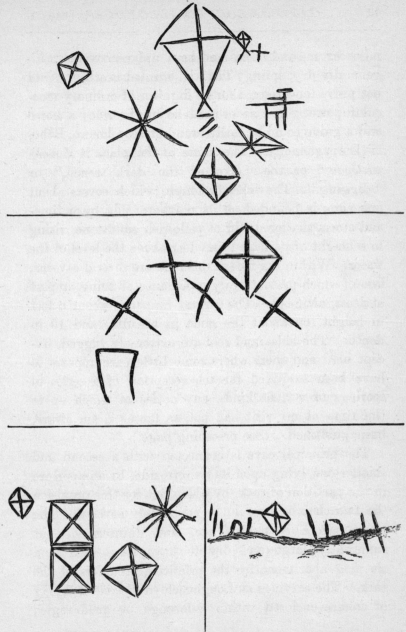

Scorings on the walls of the Cave of Loughnacloyduff, Co. Fermanagh.
(Scale, one-third.)

miles or so, and back, across an upland covered with
generally dry, springy turf and stunted heather, would
not prove too tiresome for an inquirer of ordinary mus-
cular power; in case of need he might ride; a horse
and a guide could be easily found at Knockmore, Boho,
or Derrygonnelly.   The name of the place is *Loughnacloyduff*, or the "lake of the dark trench," or
"digging."   The lake, or lough, which covers about
one acre, is bounded on its northern side by a time-
and-storm-shattered cliff of yellowish sandstone, rising
to a height of perhaps thirty feet above the level of the
water.   Within the face of this rock are several caverns,
two of which present every appearance of being, in part
at least, artificial.   The largest measures about 6 feet
in height, by about the same in breadth, and 10 in
depth.   The sides and roof are extremely rugged, except here and there where some little care appears to
have been exercised for the reception of a series of
scorings of various kinds, any notice of which up to
the time of my visit had not, as far as I am aware,
been published.   (See preceding page.)

The principal cave is connected with a second and
smaller one, lying upon its western side, by an aperture
in the partition of rock, by which but for this provision
the two chambers would be completely severed.   The
lesser cavern is small, rude, and uninscribed, but
sufficiently large and dry to have been used as a
sleeping apartment by the primitive occupiers of the
rock.   The carvings at Loughnacloyduff consist chiefly
of crosses enclosed within a lozenge or quadrangle;

of starlike designs, and of strokes which look very like a species of ogamic writing. It is probable that some of these figures may be disguised crosses.

I may state that the caverns—once perhaps the home of a family whose "young barbarians" clomb the adjacent rocks, and snared trout in the neighbouring *loch* —are now literally dens of wild animals, foxes, and brocks or badgers. The bones, and shreds of the hide, of hares, and the tattered plumage of grouse attest the successful raidings of the fox, or mᴀ'opᴀʒh-ꞁuᴀꞁö, the "red dog" of the Irish.

In other parts of Ireland besides Fermanagh caves bearing markings on their sides may be yet found; but hitherto they have escaped observation, excepting perhaps in one instance, near Ballyshannon, of which example I shall have something to say further on. Be it understood that in the foregoing observations I have referred only to natural, or partly artificial, rock-caverns, and in no instance to the souterraines, lined with dry stone masonry and roofed over with flags, found very plentifully in various parts of the country, and too carelessly or vaguely described by some writers under the title of "*caves.*" This error of nomenclature on the part of old chroniclers might be readily condoned, but modern archæologists, when noticing subterraneous works, often of inconsiderable dimensions, and built for various purposes, should call them by their proper and distinctive names—and not style them "caves," simply.

Rocking Stones.—In a field situate not far from the " Eglone," described in a former chapter, occurs a huge mass, of the same lithic character. It is known as the Rocking Stone, and, though tons in weight, may be swayed some eighteen inches on either side by very slight exertion of the hand. These so-called " rocking stones" are not uncommonly found in various parts of Ireland and Great Britain. Up to a comparatively recent period they had been supposed to have been associated in some way with the celebration of Druidical rites or mysteries. That idea is no longer held, except, perhaps, by some few old-fashioned and unreasoning people, whose minds had been impressed with the wild fancies of visionary antiquaries of the last century. Upon the borders of Fermanagh and Cavan, about three miles along the mountain road from the village of Black Lion, in the direction of the Shannon Pot, may be seen a very characteristic example of the kind of remain under notice. It consists of an immense block of stone, six feet high, somewhat globular in shape, and weighing several tons. The stone rests upon a rock, and is so poised that a moderate pressure of the fingers will suffice to move it. The position of the mass would certainly seem to be artificial. My own impression is that the stone or rock was anciently placed where it at present stands in memory of some now long forgotten hero, champion, or event—in fact that it is a gallaun, which, owing to an accidental peculiarity, existing either in its own configuration or in that of the supporting rock, may be thus shaken a few inches backwards and forwards. On the slope of a hill, on the old battle-field of Northern Moytura, in company with Colonel Wood-Martin, I came across a fine boulder, which was supposed to oscillate. We, however, failed to move it, and were informed by our guide that sometimes the stone rocked and that sometimes it was immovable; " it may," says the Colonel, "probably be stiff after heavy rains, when clay is washed down the slope, and rests in the socket on which it is balanced."

Of the other rocking stones found in Ireland it may safely be said that they are simply erratic blocks dropped into their present positions some time during the decline of the glacial age. A few of them, indeed, may have been looked upon with superstitious awe by the worshippers of stocks and stones, during the dark ages preceding the introduction of Christianity in these islands.

Druid's Chairs, or Seats — Inauguration Stones, &c. &c.—Several rude stone monuments of uncertain class occur in Ireland. The late Richard Rolt Brash, c.e., m.r.i.a., in the *Gentleman's Magazine* for April, 1865, gave an interesting article on " Ancient Chairs and Stones of Inauguration," in which he stated :—" The class of monument now under consideration has been found in countries widely apart. Examples of the stone chair in its most ancient types have been met with in Ireland, Wales, Greece, and South America." It is only to some supposed Irish

examples I shall now refer. The so-called Coronation
Chair of the O'Neills of Clandeboye, after many vicissi-
tudes and wanderings, is now preserved at Rathcarrick,
near Sligo. It consists of a rudely quadrangular block
of stone, from one side of which, slightly sloping backwards, rises a somewhat thin member, in form and size
extremely similar to the back of a seventeenth century
chair formed of oak, such as may sometimes be seen in
the humbler dwellings of persons of the farming class.
The chair, if it be a chair, is entirely of natural formation, and has evidently never been touched by a tool.
Now, as far as I am aware, there is no record to show
that in ancient times the kings or chieftains of Ireland
on the occasion of their inauguration were seated. On
the contrary they are described as standing upon a
stone, with their feet resting within or upon certain
sculptured hollows in the rock or stone, the shape of a
man's foot, and which were supposed to indicate the
shape and size of the sole of the foot of the first great
captain of the reigning race. Extremely little depen-
dence can be placed on the numerous, and sometimes
conflicting, stories which were current concerning this
" O'Neill Chair," and it may be well here to waive any
discussion concerning what is at best a very doubtful
antique.

The "Hag's Chair," on Sliabh na Callighe, one of
the Loughcrew hills, near Oldcastle, Co. Meath, has
all the appearance of being a boulder. It is one of the
great stones which formed a circle enclosing the chief
of the magnificent carns of that locality. The late

Eugene Conwell thought that he had discovered in it the judicial seat of no less a person than Ollamh Fodhla, whom he describes as "Ireland's famous monarch and law-maker, upwards of three thousand years ago"! I need now only state that Mr. Conwell does not appear to have convinced antiquaries that his identification of the stone, or that of the group of antiquities with which it is found associated, is worthy of serious consideration.

On the shore of the pilgrim-haunted Lough Derg, Co. Donegal, may be seen an enormous stone, time out of mind called "St. Brigid's Chair." It is simply a boulder, fashioned by nature into what is at present a very chair-looking object. Visible from many points in the neighbourhood of Florencecourt, Co. Fermanagh, occurs a chasm in the neighbouring mountain, called the "Giant's Seat"; but it would be tedious in a "Handbook" to refer, as might easily be done, to further examples of the exuberance of fancy shown by many of our people.

It might be well, however, if only in one instance, to explain a popular error into which not a few of our citizens have fallen. A singular pile of stones, usually called the "Druids' Judgment Seat," stands near the village of Killiney, not far from the Martello Tower, upon the opposite side of the road. It was formerly enclosed within a circle of great stones and a ditch. The former has been destroyed, and the latter so altered that little of its pristine character remains. "The Seat" is composed of large, rough granite blocks, and if really of the period to which tradition refers it, an unusual degree of care must have been exercised for its preservation. The stones bear many indications of their having been at least re-arranged at no very distant time. Small wedges have been introduced as props between the greater stones. The right arm is detached from the other part, to which it fits but clumsily. The whole, indeed, bears the appearance of

"Druids' Judgment Seat," Killiney.

a modern antique, composed of stones which once formed a portion of some ancient monument. One great evidence of its being a forgery consists in the position which it occupies near the eastern side of the enclosure, while the back of the seat is turned towards the west and towards the centre of the space anciently environed by the stone circle. The following are its dimensions:—Breadth at the base, 11½ feet; depth of the seat, 1 foot 9 inches; extreme height, 7 feet.

Of several detached stones remaining in the enclosure I have engraved one remarkable for the form into which it has been cut. It is a work probably coeval with the ancient circle, and symbolical of the sun and moon.

Ancient Inscribed Stone, Killiney.

A "Brehon's Chair," so called by Beranger, an artist and archæologist who during the latter half of the last century paid much attention to the subject of Irish antiquities, may be seen on the lands of Glensouthwell, near Hollypark, about three miles and a half from Rathfarnham, Co. Dublin. This monument has been most absurdly misnamed. It is in fact a very remarkable example of the cromleac, or dolmen, and bears no resemblance to a chair of any description. The table, or covering, which had fallen, until a few years ago lay on the ground beside it. This, unfortunately, no longer exists, the stone having been wantonly broken to pieces and used for building purposes.

The Bullàn, or Rock Basin.—Throughout Ireland, and particularly in districts of the North-west, may be observed basin-like hollows cut into the undisturbed rock, or sunk in boulders, or in the sides, or shelving portions of natural caves. In size and section they vary considerably; some examples, in extreme diameter, measuring four feet or so, while others are scarcely bigger than a small breakfast saucer. The average diameter might be estimated fourteen inches. In section they present three distinct varieties, the most usual being that of an inverse cone, while many are bowl-shaped, and not a few simply shallow depressions with vertical sides. While many theories have been promulgated as to their origin and uses, no writer has been able definitely to clear up the question. There can be no doubt that a number of our bullàns have in some way or another been associated with pagan sepulchral rites, while there seems abundant evidence to warrant a conclusion that, occasionally at least, some examples were utilized as baptismal fonts, or at any rate, as receptacles for holy water. They have been styled "mortars" by some archæologists, who imagined that they had been used for the pounding of grain or other vegetable matter. This theory is opposed by the fact that the hollow is frequently in section an equilateral triangle with a very acute lower point. It is manifest that a bullàn thus shaped could never have been intended for pounding purposes. Some examples, which are found on the vertical sides of boulders, or on the almost perpendicular face of the natural rock, could

not possibly have been designed to hold for a moment
anything like grain. Bullàns thus placed occur on a rock
at Garranbane, near Tempo, Co. Fermanagh, and on an
enormous erratic lying by the side of the road leading
from that townlet to Enniskillen, at a distance of about
one mile from the former place, two well-defined specimens appear. On a beautiful eminence in the townland
of Standingstone, within the demesne of Castlecool,
close to Enniskillen, a grand dallan, bearing at least
two bullàns, may be seen. The monument is at present
prostrate, but that it was not always so is indicated by
the name of the surrounding land. Within the great
sepulchral chambers of Newgrange, Dowth, and Sliabh
na Cailliagh, Co. Meath, are large examples; and when
exploring the pagan cemetery at Drumnakilly, near
Omagh, Co. Tyrone, it was my fortune to unearth two
bullàn stones which had sustained cinerary urns, placed
mouth downward upon them. These stones are now
deposited in the Archæological Museum of Kilkenny,
together with the fictilia referred to.

The late Rev. F. Sherman, in a note to one of his
Papers (Loca Patriciana), published in the Journal of
the Royal Historical and Archæological Association of
Ireland, p. 281, vol. iii., 4th series, gives a curious
reference to a relic of the kind under notice. *Mesgegra*,
king of Leinster in the first century of the Christian
era, is slain and decapitated by *Conal Cearnach*, the
champion of Ulster. The head is laid upon a stone,
and the tale records " that the blood flowed through it
to the ground." The stone is said still to remain in

the stream opposite the ruins of the Franciscan church
of Clane. "It is a bullàn stone, and has an inverse
conical cavity eighteen inches deep, and as many wide,
on its upper surface."

Bullàns sometimes occur singly, as in the celebrated
"Deer Stone" in Glendalough, Co. Wicklow; they
are found in pairs, as in that most curious example
at Kill-o'-the-Grange, near Blackrock, Co. Dublin;
in threes, as close to the ancient church of Temple-
naffrin, adjoining Belcoo, Co. Fermanagh; and in
numbers, up to nine. It is quite unnecessary here
to give an account of all the examples known to
occur in Ireland; and indeed, any attempt in that
direction would prove abortive, so great is their
number, and as every year the list increases. Two
very striking monuments of the class, however, must
be referred to. In the first place I mention the nine-
holed bullàn boulder, lying upon the shore of Upper
Lough MacNean, near the ancient church of Killinagh,
and in the immediate vicinity of a well called "*Tober
Brigid,*" formerly, and I believe still, held very sacred
by many of the neighbouring peasantry. It seems to
me that our bullàns, as a rule, are found curiously
associated with certain springs or wells usually esteemed
holy. The reason for the continued veneration of many
wells found in Ireland has been very happily explained
by Dr. Joyce, in his invaluable work on Irish *Place-
Names :* "After the general spread of the Faith the
people's affection for wells was not only retained, but
intensified ; for most of the early preachers of the

Gospel established their humble foundations — many
of them destined to grow, in after years, into great
religious and educational institutions — beside those
fountains whose waters at the same time supplied the
daily wants of the little communities, and served for
the baptism of converts. In this manner most of our
early saints became associated with wells, hundreds of
which still retain the names of the holy men who con-
verted and baptized the pagan multitudes on their
margins."

CHAPTER II.

SEPULCHRAL REMAINS, CISTS—THE CROMLEAC, GIANT'S GRAVE, OR DOLMEN—CARNS, AND MOUNDS, ETC.

REAT interest has of late years been
attached to the subject of early burial
usages in Erin.—The pagan Irish appear
to have made use of two modes of sepulture, viz., by interring the body whole,
in a horizontal or perpendicular position,
and by cremation. In the latter practice, when the remains had become sufficiently calcined, the ashes were
placed in an urn of clay or stone, which was then deposited within an artificial chamber formed of uncemented
stones. Over the smaller chambers or cists it appears to
have been customary to raise a carn, or an earthen
mound. Cinerary urns, however, have been found
within the area of stone circles, and frequently in the
plain ground, simply inclosed in a small cist, or turned
mouth downward upon a slate. They have also been
discovered in tumuli, not many feet from the surface;
even in mounds that in their centre contained other,
and probably much more ancient, deposits. In case of
interment, the grave appears generally to have been
formed of flags, often of considerable size, placed edge-

ways and enclosing a space barely sufficient to contain
the body; over these similar stones were placed, the
whole lying a little beneath the surface of the earth.

A most interesting account of burial in an upright
position is referred to in the Book of Armagh, where
King Loeghaire is represented as telling St. Patrick
that his father Niall used exhort him never to believe
in Christianity, but to retain the ancient religion of his
ancestors, and to be interred in the Hill of Tara, like a
man standing up in battle, and with his face turned to
the south, as if bidding defiance to the men of Leinster.

A question, which to a comparatively recent period
had been rather warmly discussed by not a few writers,
was one referring to the cromleac—its character, uses,
and so forth. The question has, I apprehend, been
sufficiently solved, and the quondam irrepressible
Druids cannot be any longer credited with the erection
of several hundreds of so-called "altars," or "temples,"
distributed all over our island; which works, from the
gigantic, chambered carns, like those of Newgrange
and Dowth, to the simplest cist (all varieties of the
cromleac idea), have been found to be merely graves
of a primitive people.

The cromleac is usually styled "*dolmen*" by English
and Continental writers. Our peasantry, however, as
a rule, call them "giants' graves," or not unfrequently, when bent on story-telling and speaking in
Irish, *Leaba Diarmida agus Graine*, or the beds of
Dermot and Graine, from two historical personages who,
according to an old legendary romance, eloped together,

and flying through the country for a year and a day, erected these " beds" wherever they rested for a night. The lady was no less a person than the betrothed wife of Fin Mac Coul, the Fingal of Mac Pherson, from whom our modern Fenians derived their name. He was a man of note in his day, in fact, commander-in-chief of the National Militia of Ireland. Graine, or Grace, was daughter of king Cormac Mac Art, who lived about the middle of the third century, A.D., and her partner in guilt was Diarmaid O'Duibhne, of whom several stories are still current. According to this legend there should be just 366 cromleacs, or " beds," in Ireland—but there is no truth in the story, which is nevertheless of some interest, as it connects the monuments with mythical, and, in Ireland, pre-Christian events. In parts of the north and west of the country they are sometimes styled " griddles."

The ordinary giant's grave, cromleac, or dolmen, when perfect, or nearly so, consists of three or more stones, unhewn, and generally so arranged as to form a small enclosure. Over these a large and usually thick stone is placed, the whole forming a kind of vault or rude chamber.

In some cases the covering seems to have slipped from its ancient position, and will be found with one end or side resting upon the ground. Du Noyer was of opinion that this was the original arrangement in many examples, the builders having failed in their efforts to raise the ponderous " table," or covering stone, or to procure suitable supporters. The position of the

upper stone, or roof, is usually sloping, but its degree
of inclination does not seem to have been regulated by
any intention or design.   This general disposition of
the "table" has been largely seized upon by advocates
of the "Druids' Altar" theory, as a proof of the sound-
ness of their opinion that these monuments were erected
for the purpose of human sacrifice.   Some enthusiastic
dreamers have gone so far as to discover in the hollows
worn by the rains and storms of centuries on the upper
surface of these venerable stones, channels artificially
excavated, for the purpose of facilitating the passage
of a victim's blood earthwards!

It is absolutely certain that only very few of the
giants' graves, or dolmens, of Ireland were at any time
covered by a carn or mound.   Our remains of this
class are, almost invariably, of what has been termed
"the free standing" order.   Mr. G. A. Lebour, in
"Nature," May 9th, 1872, presents some very interesting remarks bearing upon the character of the
principal dolmens and cist-bearing mounds of Finis-
terre. He states that "in most cases in that department
the dolmens occupy situations in every respect similar
to those in which the tumuli are found, so that meteor-
ological, and indeed every other but human, agencies
must have affected both in the same manner and
degree. Notwithstanding this, the dolmens are invariably bare, and the cists are as constantly covered;
there are no signs of even incipient degradation and
denudation in the latter, and none of former covering
in the first."   These remarks apply in all their force

to groups of similar remains which are to be found in
Ireland. A few instances out of many may be here
referred to. About two miles and a-half from the
village of Black Lion, in the county of Cavan, but on
the borders of Fermanagh, may be seen two truly
magnificent " giants' graves," the larger of which,
measuring forty-seven feet in length, by about ten in
breadth, remains in a complete state of preservation.
Five flagstones, some of considerable thickness, closely
cover this enormous work, which, it should be observed, was, and partially still is, enclosed by an oval
line of standing stones, some of which have fallen,
while others, in number and position sufficient to convey an idea of the original plan, remain *in situ*. At
one end occurs a small but apparently undisturbed
stone circle, an examination of which, by competent
explorers, might lead to some very curious antiquarian
discoveries. At a little distance stand a cromleac (the
covering stone of which measures fifteen feet, five
inches in length by fifteen in breadth), another dolmen,
besides a considerable number of dallans or pillar stones.
In the immediate vicinity occurs a fine chambered carn,
which but for the operation of rabbit-hunting boys would
now stand complete. The chamber, or cist, was found
to contain a fine cinerary urn. The question suggests
itself, why should this cist-bearing carn remain almost
perfect, while the neighbouring megaliths, if they were
ever mound-enclosed, are found cleanly and completely
bare ? Again, at the " Barr " of Fintona we find two
important carns remaining almost completely pre-

served ; while close at hand is a giant's grave which, if ever covered, is now most entirely denuded.

Many absurd observations in connexion with our cromleacs have from time to time been made. For instance, Mr. Fergusson, in the section of his voluminous work devoted to a description of Irish megalithic remains, makes the following extraordinary statement :—"It is extremely difficult to write anything regarding the few solitary dolmens of Ireland. Not that their history could not be, perhaps, easily ascertained, but simply because everyone has hitherto been content to consider them as pre-historic, and no one has consequently given himself the trouble to investigate the matter." Now, the fact is that Ireland, instead of possessing only a few solitary dolmens, happens to be the richest country in the world in that class of monument. Irish archæologists are not sufficiently demented as to go searching for the history of remains which, upon being dug into, almost invariably present calcined bones, sepulchral urns more or less perfect, and objects, instruments, and personal ornaments, composed of stone, flint, bone, or shell. We know that in our very oldest manuscripts not one single allusion to the practice of cremation can be found. It must have been in disuse for ages before the time of St. Patrick, and even the use of "giants' graves" as places of interment appears to have been out of date long before the beginning of the fifth century, A.D.

In reference to this subject generally it may be

observed that, according to Colgan, dolmens appear
even so long ago as the time of St. Patrick to have been
robed in mystery.   In his " Tour in Connaught" the
late Rev. Cæsar Otway gives the following translation
of what appears to be the ·earliest notice of a " giant's
grave" extant:—"On a certain day, as St. Patrick
was going about preaching the Gospel and healing all
manner of disease, he met by the wayside a tomb of
astonishing size (being thirty feet long).   His com-
panions observing this, expressed their opinion that
no man could ever have arrived at such a size as to
require such a grave.   Whereupon the saint replied
that God, by the resurrection of the giant, could per-
suade them, provided they were not altogether slow
of faith.   For just at that time there existed much
doubt respecting the truth of the general resurrection.
St. Patrick, therefore, prayed fervently that his state-
ments might be borne out by facts, and that thereby the
scruples of doubt might be eradicated from their minds.
And lo! a wonder—wonder heretofore in past ages un-
heard of.   For the man of heavenly might approaches
the sepulchre; he pours out his powerful prayer; signs
with the staff of Jesus the tomb.   And up rose the
giant from the grave; and there he stood before them
all, in stature and countenance most horrible; and
looking intently on St. Patrick, and weeping most
dolorously, he cried, 'Immense gratitude I owe you,
my lord and master, beloved of God, and elect; because
that at least for one hour you have snatched me from
the gates of hell, where I have been suffering unspeak-

able torments.' And he besought the saint that he would allow him to follow him; but the saint refused, giving for his reason that men could not bear to look without intolerable terror on his countenance. When being asked who he was, he said his name was Glarcus, son of Chais; that heretofore he was swineherd to king Laogair, and that about one hundred years ago he was attacked and killed by one Fin Mac Coul, in the reign of king Cairbre. St. Patrick then advised him to believe in the Triune God, and be baptized, if he would not return to his place of torment, to which the giant joyfully agreed; and then he returned to his grave, and he was delivered, according to the word of the saint, from his place of suffering."—Colgan, "Trias Thaum.," Sexta Vita Pat., page 83.

Cromleacs and kindred monuments of a (with us) pre-historic age are very numerous in Co. Dublin.

The Phœnix Park Cists or Tombs. — The ancient sepulchre situated in the Phœnix Park, a little to the west of the Hibernian School, was discovered in the year 1838 by some workmen employed under the Commissioners of Woods and Forests, in the removal of an ancient tumulus, which measured in circumference 120 feet, and in height 15 feet. During the progress of the work, four stone cists (*kistvaens*), each enclosing an urn of baked clay, within which were calcined bones, ashes, &c. One of these urns, which is now in the Museum of the Royal Irish Academy, was fortunately saved in a nearly perfect state by Captain Larcom, of the Royal Engineers. When the labourers had come upon the tomb, the works were stopped at the request of Captain Larcom, in order that a deputation from the Academy might assemble on the spot for the purpose of collecting and reporting upon facts relating to the discovery. The tomb at present consists of seven stones set in the ground, in the form of an irregular oval, three of which support a table, or covering stone, which measures in length 6 feet 6 inches; in breadth, at the

Tomb or Cist, Phœnix Park.

broadest part, 3 feet 6 inches; and in thickness between 14 and 16 inches. The spaces between the stones which formed the enclosure were filled with others of smaller size, which, since the discovery, have fallen out or been removed. The following is an extract from the report of the Academy:—"In the recess they enclosed two perfect male human skeletons were found, and also the tops of the femora of another, and a single bone of an animal, supposed to be that of a dog. The heads of the skeletons rested to the north, and as the enclosure is not of sufficient extent to have permitted the bodies to lie at full length, they must have been bent at the vertebræ, or at the lower joints. In both skulls the teeth are nearly perfect, but the molars were more worn in one than in the other. Immediately under each skull was found collected together a considerable quantity of small shells common on our coasts, and known to conchologists by the name of *Nerita littoralis*. On examination these shells were found to have been rubbed down on the valve with a stone to make a second hole, for the purpose, as it appeared evident, of their being strung to form necklaces; and a vegetable fibre, serving this purpose, was also discovered, a portion of which was through the shells. A small fibula of bone, and a knife, or arrowhead, of flint, were also found."

It is greatly to be regretted that a monument so well calculated, at some period—perhaps not far distant, when the Irish people, as a body, shall see in their antiquities something more than curiosities—to awaken a desire in the minds of those who may visit it for further instruction, should be suffered to remain a prey to every wanderer in the Park desirous of possessing a "piece of the tomb," in order to show it as a wonder; and if steps be not taken to preserve this most interesting remain from the hands of such plunderers, it is likely to suffer the fate of other monuments presently to be adverted to.

The skulls, necklace, urns, &c., of this valuable "find" may be seen in the collection of the Royal

Irish Academy, now deposited in our National Museum, Kildare-street, Dublin.

Visitors to the Phœnix Park will find in the grounds of the Royal Zoological Gardens a cist, or diminutive cromleac, in many respects similar to that just noticed, which was discovered some years ago in a sandpit immediately adjoining the neighbouring village of Chapelizod. This monument, though not occupying its ancient position, and, notably, a restoration, should be seen by students of Irish antiquities, the stones of which it is composed having been carefully replaced in their original order. It is on record that within this tomb a human skeleton was found, but no mention of anything else it may have contained has been preserved.

Howth Cromleac.—This fine monument is situate near the base of an inland cliff, within the grounds of Howth Castle, and at a distance of about three-quarters of a mile from the sea shore. It consists, at present, of ten blocks of quartz, of which the table or covering stone, the largest, measures from north to south eighteen, and from east to west nineteen and a-half feet, the extreme thickness being eight feet. The weight of this mass has been computed at ninety tons. Such an enormous pressure appears to have caused the supporters more or less to give way: they all incline eastward, and the table would seem to have slipped in that direction, in its course breaking one of the pillars in two. It did not come to the ground, however, having been arrested in its descent by the undisturbed stump of the fractured stone upon which, in an inclined position, it now reposes at its lowest edge. The supporters are about six feet and a-half in height, so that, as Beranger, who visited and described the remains about a hundred years ago, states :—"This, one of the grandest mausoleums, must have made a noble figure standing, as the tallest man might stand and walk under it with ease."

Howth Cromleac.

The work on the interior would seem to have constituted an irregular chamber, tending east and west; but much disturbance of the stones has occurred, and it would be now impossible by drawings and plans to give a very reliable idea of the original appearance of this still grandly impressive pile, which, I may add, appears never to have been surmounted by carn or tumulus of any kind. These stones were formerly called " Fin Mac Coul's Quoits."

Kilternan Cromleac.—This is another wonderful work of its class, when we consider the approximate

weight of its table—eighty tons—and the difficulty as
we must suppose, of raising, in a rude age, such a mass
upon supporters. The covering stone, like all others
of this monument, is of the granite of the district.   Its
measurements are :—Extreme length, 23 feet 6 inches ;
extreme breadth, 17 feet : greatest thickness, 6 feet
6 inches ; weight estimated 80 tons. The supporters
vary in height from 2 to 4 feet, but without expensive

Kilternan Cromleac.

and probably hazardous digging, it is impossible to
know how far they may be sunk below the present
ground level. Some considerable disturbance in their
arrangement appears to have occurred. Several would
seem to have subsided, but the roof is still supported
on pillars ; and the height of the enclosure may be
stated as about five feet from floor to roof. The plan
of chamber is very irregular—it may be described as

extending east and west. This cromleac is known as
" The Giant's Grave," but there is no story connected
with it, folklore in this district having generations ago
ceased to exist.

Kilternan is situate near the Golden Ball village,
about seven miles from Dublin, and as the "crow
flies" about three from the sea. A walk of about
two miles from Carrickmines station, on the Dublin,
Wicklow and Wexford line of railway would bring
a visitor to the place.

Mount Venus Cromleac.—This monument is no
longer nearly perfect. Its table, having evidently
slipped from its original position, is at present sup-

Mount Venus Cromleac.

ported by a single stone about six feet in height, and
of considerable massiveness. The remains indicate the
former rude grandeur of the structure, the covering
stone measuring 19½ feet in length, by 11½ in breadth,
and 5 in thickness. Several of the former supporting

stones would seem to have been removed, and others
have evidently been broken. The material is granite,
of a very hard, close, and durable description. It
seems to have weathered very little, all its remaining
stones presenting angles of considerable sharpness.

Du Noyer was of opinion that this cromleac was of
what he styled the "earth-fast" class, and that the
roof had always in part rested upon the ground. In
this supposition O'Neill, no mean authority on such
matters, did not by any means coincide. The weight
of the covering stone is supposed to be about seventy
tons. So great a pressure might well cause some of
the weaker supporters to give way, in which case the
pile would very probably assume its present appearance.
It is not in the least likely that this tomb had at any
time been covered by a tumulus or carn. It is situate
at a distance of two miles and a-half in an inland
direction from the village of Rathfarnham. Distance
from the sea about five miles. On account of disturbance of the stones it would be now impossible to
make a plan of the chamber.

Shanganagh Cromleac.—At Shanganagh, not
far from the hamlet of Loughlinstown, may be seen
a very fine specimen of what may be styled, as regards
size, a cromleac of the second class. It is supported
upon four stones, and presents no appearance of having
been enveloped in a mound of any description. Like
nearly every one of its kindred remains in the county
of Dublin it is formed of granite blocks. The covering

stone measures 9 feet in length, by 7 at its greatest
breadth; it is 3½ feet in its extreme thickness; and its
highest portion is at present slightly over 9 feet above
the ground; weight about twelve tons.   The chamber

Shanganagh Cromleac.

would seem to extend east and west.   There is neither
name nor legend in connexion with this monument,
which may be easily visited from Killiney railway
station.   The situation is close to the sea.

Druid's Glen Cromleac.—Situate in a picturesque valley close to Cabinteely, Co. Dublin, stands
a very perfect cromleac.   This monument may be
reached in a short walk from the Carrickmines station
of the Dublin, Wicklow, and Wexford Railway.

The site is a little over one mile and a-half from the
sea coast. The covering stone is of an irregular form,
but the under portion, which forms the top of the chamber, is quite flat and horizontal. The following are its
dimensions:—Length and breadth, 15 feet; extreme
thickness, slightly more than 3 feet. It would not be

Druid's Glen Cromleac.

easy to calculate the weight of this mass, on account of
the irregularity of form which the block presents ; but
it may be roughly estimated at about 60 tons. The
material is granite. A number of detached stones
lying about this very perfect example would indicate
that it was originally accompanied by a circle of pillar
stones.

Cromleac and so-called "Druid's Judgment Seat" near Hollypark, Rathfarnham.—Upwards of a hundred years ago Beranger wrote as follows :— "Druid's Chair.—This piece of antiquity, the only one yet discovered, is situated at the foot of the Three-Rock Mountain. It is supposed to be the seat of judgment of the Arch-Druid, from whence he delivered his oracles. It has the form of an easy chair wanting the seat, and is composed of three rough, unhewn stones, about 7 feet high, all clear above ground. How deep they are in the earth remains unknown. Close to it is a sepulchral monument, or cromleac, supposed to be the tomb of the Arch-Druid. It is 15 feet in girth, and stands on three supporters, about 2 feet high, and is planted round with trees. The top stone is 8½ feet long." The so-called "chair" still remains, and the above account fairly describes it. But it never was a chair. It is evidently a rather small and tall cromleac that has lost its covering stone. Of the "cromleac" noticed by Beranger I could find no trace, but the ground in the neighbourhood of the "chair" is now so covered with scrub and other vegetation that a structure only two feet in height might readily be lost to view amongst the brambles and weeds. The "chair," or "judgment seat," stands just outside the wall of Hollypark demesne, and quite close to the College of St. Columba.

Supposed Megalith on the Three-Rock Mountain, Co. Dublin.—Anyone familiar with the scenery

round Dublin will readily remember the appearance of
the Three-Rock Mountain. This is the nearest commanding eminence to the metropolis. It rises in a
gentle slope from near Dundrum, a village four miles
from the General Post-office, and two miles further on,
upon its summit, stand three distinct groups of rocks,
which from a distance present all the appearance of
carns. These, however, were never raised by human
hands; their interest is entirely of a geological character, and they need not have been here mentioned
had not Beranger enumerated one of them amongst
the so-called "Druidical remains" of the county;
and had he not only drawn them, and described
them in terms which have been quoted as worthy
of consideration by a writer in the pages of our
leading Archæological Journal.

Glencullen Cromleac.—This mausoleum is situated on the eastern side of Glencullen, not far from
Kilternan, in a very wild district, extending to the
west of the Three-Rock Mountain, and at a distance
of some three miles, in a direct line, from the sea. It
is the only monument noticed in this account of our
Dublin megaliths which I have not personally visited
and measured. It is described by O'Neill as having
"a roof rock 10 feet long, 8 feet broad, and 4 feet
thick, extreme measures." "The longest direction,"
he states, "of the roof rock is W. S.W., or nearly
E. and W. The chamber is greatly damaged."

Shankill Cromleac.—In Cromwell's "Excursions through Ireland," vol. iii., p. 159, there is an engraving, after a drawing by Petrie of a dolmen at this place, which is situate about four miles to the north or north-west of Bray, at a distance of a couple of miles from the nearest shore of the sea. O'Neill writes, in 1852, that he could not find it, and heard that it had been removed a few years previously. Nevertheless the monument still exists, and was seen and sketched by myself a couple of years ago. It stands by the side of a road leading across the eastern slope of Carrigollagher, in the direction of Rathmichael, and presents a very fair specimen of its class. Though much ruined it retains its covering stone *in situ;* this stands so high that a tall man, without bending, may freely walk beneath it.

Before parting with the subject of dolmens as found in the vicinity of Dublin, I may remark it as a curious fact that in the east of Ireland such remains are almost, if not invariably, of the free-standing and uncovered class. The tombs noticed as occurring in the Phœnix Park should, I presume, be classified with the cist, not the dolmen proper. If we want to find accompaniments we must seek for them much further north, or in districts of the west or south-west of Ireland, where Colonel Wood-Martin has had the fortune to be the first to notice some most interesting varieties. It was certainly well known that in the county of Sligo scores of sub-aerial giants' graves are to be found

environed by one or more lines of stones, which are
not unfrequently associated with free-standing pillar
stones, and, as would sometimes seem, with incipient
alignments. But until the appearance of "Rude Stone
Monuments of Sligo and Achill" it was not known that
in the west existed T-shaped sepulchres; and others,
in plan like a dumb-bell, the handle representing the
grave, while the bulbous ends might be expressed in
the form of regularly-constructed stone circles. He
was also enabled to point to triangular graves, a form
in mortuary construction, in Ireland, hitherto, I believe,
only described in his most valuable work.

"It is remarkable," observes Colonel Wood-Martin,
"that, in the county of Sligo, the characteristic features
of the megaliths varied according to districts: for example, in Carrowmore the circular form was almost
universal, whereas in Northern Carbury an oblong
arrangement appears to predominate. Again, in the
Deerpark Monument, the general architectural prin-
ciples displayed at Stonehenge can be traced.

"Cremations and bodily interments have been found
intermixed in a manner to lead to the belief that both
forms of burial prevailed contemporaneously. Urns
to contain the ashes of the dead were, possibly, used
as a special mark of honour; also, perhaps, to facilitate
the conveyance of the human remains from a distance
to the chosen place of interment. In a country wherein
were thick woods and long stretches of bog to be tra-
versed, the passage of funeral processions must have
been attended with delays and difficulties.

" In many instances so great an amount of charcoal remains have been discovered that there seems reason to believe the bodies were burned at the place of sepulture ; and from the quantity of animal bones found intermixed with the human, it cannot but be inferred that an ample supply of ' funeral-baked meats ' was provided for those who attended the obsequies.

" Amongst the Irish peasantry the custom still survives of providing refreshment, not merely for persons who are present at the place of interment, but for friends and neighbours who assemble to watch at night beside the corpse during the intervals occurring between the dates of death and burial ; and these ' wakes ' (as they are called), although supposed to betoken respect for the dead, are often scenes of unseemly feasting and carousing.

" Climate, the productions of the country in which they dwell, and the habits of life thereby engendered, influence strongly the character and acts of a people ; and although the general instinctive feeling of primitive man led him to honour the last resting-place of his dead, yet the memorials thus erected necessarily depend upon the kind of material at hand available for the purpose. The geological nature of the surroundings must be taken into consideration, not merely with regard to megalithic structures, but also to cashels, some of which, according to the districts in which they were found, had been constructed with stones of very small size, whilst in other instances the stones were of greater magnitudes."

A considerable number of our larger giants' graves
bear great resemblance to several found in the Channel
Islands and in Brittany.   One of the more remarkable
of these occurring in the eastern portion of Ireland
may be seen near the northern extremity of the parish
of Monasterboice, Co. Louth.   It is called by the
neighbouring people the house or tomb of Calliagh
Vera, or Birra, a mythic witch, whose name is
associated with several wild legends referring to the
mysterious carns and other antiquities remaining upon
the hills of Loughcrew, near Oldcastle.   The work is
free-standing, and has evidently never been covered
by a carn or mound; it is roughly oblong in form,
extending exactly east and west, and measuring, internally, 12 feet 6 inches in length, by 4 feet at one
end, and 3 at the other, in breadth.   Of the supposed
former inhabitant of this "house" I shall have presently a little to say.

At Greenmount, about five miles further to the
north, some years ago General Lefroy opened an
earthen mound, which was found to contain a very
similar chamber, the measurements of which were
21 feet by 4, the height being 5 feet.   The roof was
formed of five very large flagstones.   I have mentioned
these two monuments as typical examples of the covered
and uncovered graves of the larger sort found in Ireland; I mean, of course, as distinguished from the
gigantic carns such as can be pointed to in various
parts of the country, some of which it will be necessary
for the purposes of this handbook presently to describe.

I may here refer to a very curious and painful story, which appears in more than one of our most reliable manuscript authorities, relating to the murder of a Bishop Cellagh, great grandson of Dathy, last pagan monarch of Ireland, by his four foster brothers, who are said to have been ecclesiastical students. For this crime the four *Maols*, as the culprits were styled (the name of each commencing with that prefix, which may be interpreted "*servant of*"), were executed upon a hill near Ballina, known as *Ard-na-Riagh*, or "the Height of the Executions."

No one will probably dispute the fact of this murder, or that, as stated, the unhappy youths were executed and buried on the spot named ; but who can say for certain that the dolmen now standing there was erected to their memory ? No doubt they had been excommunicated and pronounced unworthy of Christian association, here and hereafter. But the bodies must be disposed of, and what is more likely to have occurred than that they were ignominiously thrust into a pagan mausoleum which had stood on the Hill of Execution from time immemorial ? Who would dream of erecting a ponderous cromleac to enclose and shelter the remains of sacrilegious murderers !

Before finally leaving the subject of the ordinary cromleac, it is well that I should notice at least four examples which bear markings, seemingly carved with some intention.

The first to be described occurs at a place called *Cloughtogle*, "the lifted stone," situated close to the

village of Lisbellaw, Co. Fermanagh. It consists of
four great stones, two of which form the sides, and one
the end, of a quadrangular chamber. On the front of
the fourth stone, which constitutes the covering, or
" table," are four well-marked cups, averaging 1¾ inch
in diameter. These are placed in a horizontal line,
extending over a space of 18 inches, and slightly
diminishing in size from left to right. The block on
which they occur is 7 feet 4 inches in length, by 5 feet
5 inches in breadth, the thickness being 2 feet.

An inscription, if it be an inscription, almost perfectly similar, may be observed on one of the upright
stones of a ruined cromleac standing on the slope of
Slievemore, island of Achill, amongst other remains,
styled on the ordnance sheet tumulus, cromleac, Danish
ditch, &c., respectively. It is difficult to imagine that
the likeness between these two sets of cup markings is
accidental. A similar array of four cups, but placed
vertically, may be seen on one of the enormous
stones forming the right-hand side of the gallery
leading into the great carn of Newgrange.

The inscribed cromleac of Lennan, or Tullycorbet,
Co. Monaghan, stands upon a knoll called by the
people of the district *Cruck-na-clia*, which may be very
well translated "Battle Hill." This monument, a fine
one of its class, presents every appearance of having
always been free-standing. It bears some extremely
curious markings, into the character of which the late
Sir Samuel Ferguson made very exhaustive inquiries ;
but on this occasion his care seems to have been thrown

away, and where Sir Samuel failed it is not likely future investigators will fare better, unless indeed by the aid of a key, of the existence of which nothing at present is known.

The Castlederg Inscribed Cromleac.—" The Castlederg cromleac," writes Sir Samuel, " will be found marked as ' Druids' Altar' on the Ordnance map of Tyrone, sheet 16, a short three-quarters of a mile to the north of the town of Castlederg, 140 yards to the east of the old Strabane road, leading through Churchtown townland. It stands on the land of Mr. Walsh, by whom the principal cap-stone was dislodged, so far as I could gather, some ten years ago. It appears that the structure had previously been rendered insecure by a stone-mason, who had abstracted one of the supporters for building purposes ; and it was suggested that the motive for casting down the cap-stone was an apprehension lest the owner's cattle, in rubbing or sheltering under it, might do themselves a mischief. That the inscription was there at the time of the first disclosure of the upper face of the support on which it is sculptured, is the common and constant statement of the people of the country ; but the case rests more satisfactorily on the fact, wholly independent of testimony, that a collateral covering stone remains *in situ*, and that the line of scorings is prolonged underneath it into a position too contracted for the use of a graving tool."

The work here consists of a continuous series of

straight scorings, accompanied by a number of dots
or depressions more or less circular in form. There
can be no doubt that a generic resemblance may be
noticed between them and many of the markings of the
Lennan inscription. This, if there were nothing more,
would raise a serious doubt of their being merely accidental or capricious indentations; "but," continues Sir
Samuel, "in fact there exist in a great number of
localities in Ireland, and in one place in North Wales,
inscribed scorings so evidently of the same nature that
it is very difficult to withhold our belief from their claim
to be regarded as significant marks."

The great majority of such irregular scorings should,
nevertheless, be looked upon with suspicion. Those
which occur on the pillar stone at Kilnasaggart, Co.
Armagh, though long considered to be Ogam characters, are now universally pronounced to be nothing
more than markings made by persons who utilized the
menhir as a block for the sharpening and pointing of
tools or weapons. The same remark applies in full
force to certain scorings and scratches which disfigure
a grand dallan standing close to the railway station
of Kesh, Co. Fermanagh, on the right-hand side of
the line as you face towards Bundoran. They are
found abundantly on the coping stones of the walls
of Londonderry, and indeed in other localities too numerous to mention. At Killowen, Co. Cork, they occur
on a stone most significantly called *clock na n'arm*, or
the (*sharpening*) *stone of the weapons*.

CHAPTER III.

PRIMITIVE FUNERAL RITES.

o speculate on the style of rites and celebrations practised on the occasion of grand funeral gatherings in connexion with the several royal cemeteries of Ireland during days of the older or later paganism, would be vain and useless. Fortunately, however, in a few of our most venerable manuscripts, which there is reason to believe are but transcripts of documents still considerably more ancient, we find some light thrown upon the subject of ante-Christian burials in Erin; For instance, see the following extract from the "Book of Lismore," given by the Bishop of Limerick in his "Notes on the Ogam Beithluisnin"*:—

"We, the Fiann," said Cailte, "both high and low, great and small, king and knight, raised a loud shout of lamentation for the brave and valiant champions. And a mound was dug for each of them; and they were put into them. Their tombstones were raised

* *Hermathena*, vol. iii.

over their graves, and their Ogam names were written
there."* See again from an account of the battle of
Gabhra, which was fought A. D. 283. The reference
appears in the Book of Leinster,† and is after all but a
copy of much older writing :—

> " An Ogam in a *lia*, a *lia* over a *leacht*,
>   In a place whither men went to battle,
>   The son of the king of Erin fell there,
>   Slain by a sharp spear on his white steed.

> " That Ogam which is upon the stone,
>   Around which the heavy hosts have fallen
>   If the heroic Finn had lived,
>   Long would that Ogam be remembered."

In an account of the death of Fiachra, son of
Eochaidh Muighmhedhoin, and brother to Niall of
the Nine Hostages, which appears in the Book of
Ballymote, the following curious story is given:—
" Then the men of Munster gave him battle in Caen-
raigne, and Maidhi Meascoragh wounded Fiachra mor-
tally in the battle. Nevertheless, the men of Munster
and the Erneans were defeated by dint of fighting, and
suffered great slaughter. Then Fiachra carried away
fifty hostages out of Munster, together with his tribute
in full, and set forth on his march to Temor. Now,
when he had reached Forraidh in Uibh Maccuais, in
West Meath, Fiachra died of his wound. His grave
was made, and his mound was raised, and his *cluiche
cainte* (funeral rites, including games and dirges),
were ignited, and his Ogam name was written, and

---

* Book of Lismore, fol. 121, *b*.   † H. 2. 18, fol. 109, *b, a*.

the hostages which had been brought from the south were buried alive round Fiachra's grave."

But that it has so often been given I might here quote at length an account of the death and burial of Fothadh Airgthech, who was killed in the battle of Ollarba, fought, according to the "Annals of the Four Masters," in the year 285 A. D. The record concludes by stating :—" And there is a pillar stone on the carn ; and an Ogam is (inscribed) on the end of the pillar stone, which is in the earth. And what is on it is Eochaid Airgthech here."*

Aughascribbagh Ogam Stone. — At a place called Aughascribbagh, situate at a little distance from the sub-post-office of Broughderg, Co. Tyrone, may be seen a monument, which with its belongings is of considerable interest, as bearing upon the pagan character of no small number of kindred remains in Ireland. It is simply a pillar stone, or menhir, of yellow sandstone, nearly square in plan, and measuring in height above ground 4 feet. Its dimensions at the base are 1 foot 6 inches by 1 foot 7 inches. The stone gradually narrows towards the top. The *ulaidh* from which it rises is now of rather small proportions, and has evidently been encroached upon by the farming operations of ages. The pillar bears upon its south-east angle an array of well-marked Ogam characters, which would seem to constitute the whole of the inscription as originally cut or punched. The letters are ⊥⊥ⱁ⊥⊥ⱁ⊔⊥⊥⊔⊔⊥⊥ⱀ⊥⊔⊔ :

* Leabhar na h-Uidhre, fol. 133, *b. b.*

the exact mode in which the scores were executed is
at present, owing to the partial weathering of the
stone, difficult to determine. The majority of the
strokes measure, as nearly as possible, $3\frac{1}{4}$ inches in
length; but, in one of the spaces, three notches,
representing the vowel *u* in the Roman alphabet, are
little more than dots. An oblique score, crossing the
angle of the stone, and measuring $6\frac{1}{2}$ inches in length,
indicates the letter *m* in the Ogam style. The inscription is $21\frac{1}{2}$ inches in length, and would seem to com-
mence at the base.

Sir Samuel Ferguson, to whose judgment I submitted a careful drawing and rubbing of the scorings,
was kind enough to reply as follows:—" Your Aughascribbagh Ogam is quite a new contribution. If you
are right in your transcript, as I dare say you are, it
is another proof of the existence of cryptic varieties.
Having no phonetic force in the ordinary equivalents,
its expression of sound, not to speak of meaning—
though it is probably a proper name—must be looked
for through a key not yet discovered."

The *ulaidh*, or carn, from which the pillar rises,
has, as already stated, all the appearance of having
been sadly denuded and encroached upon. It is composed chiefly of small stones, and now measures about
seven or eight feet in diameter.

Here, then, at Aughascribbagh we find an Ogam-
bearing monument which exhibits all the features
of a pagan tomb, as described in our oldest literary
remains. But this is not all. Just immediately

adjoining stands a menhir, or dallan, about fourteen feet in height, and of enormous breadth and thickness—a memorial, indeed, of a kind which it was not the custom of any Christian community to upraise. Upon the brow of the hill, immediately facing these two "sentinels of time," occurs a magnificent and very perfect stone circle. No indication of ancient Christian occupation remains about this interesting spot, the aspect of which is impressively weird and pagan. The neighbouring people, who are few in number, accept the usual tradition in connexion with such monuments, that these stones were placed as they now stand by giants !

Toppid Mountain Ogam Stone. — It would appear from the Brehon Laws that Ogam-inscribed stones were sometimes placed in mounds, where they might be referred to as authorities, defining the mearings of territories or landed possessions. Such mounds, or carns, may possibly have been long in use as pagan sepulchres. An interesting example of what appears to be a flag of this class was discovered in the summer of 1875, amongst material removed a yard or so from the great carn which crowns the summit of Toppid Mountain, near Enniskillen. All the particulars of this "find" were contributed by me to the *Journal* of the Royal Historical and Archæological Association of Ireland, for October of that year. By the kindness of the committee of that institution I am enabled here to

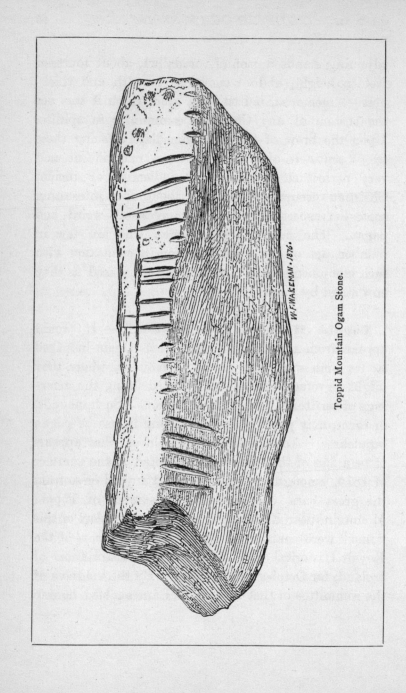

W.F.WAKEMAN. 1876.

Toppid Mountain Ogam Stone.

give an illustration of the *leac*, which accompanied the Paper referred to.

The flag measures 1 ft. 6 in., by $8\frac{3}{4}$ in., and is of red sandstone. It is $3\frac{3}{4}$ in. in its greatest, and $2\frac{1}{2}$ in. in its smallest thickness. The inscription plainly reads: ⊤⊤⊤⊤ ⌁⌁⌁⌁ ⌁⌁⌁ ⌁⌁⌁ ⌁⌁⌁⌁ ⌁⌁⌁, "NETTACU," and is evidently complete in itself, the ends of the stone being rounded and timeworn, presenting not the least appearance of having been fractured since the time the legend was cut. Nettacu was almost certainly the name of a man. The original form of the patronymic may have been somewhat shorter, viz. *Netcu*, the Ogam scribes being in the habit of adding a syllable or so to a name, in order to increase its dignity of appearance.

In the Aughascribbagh and Toppid Mountain Ogams we have, it would seem, unmistakably pagan examples of that mode of writing. But, as Bishop Graves has shown, several of our early Christian memorial stones bear inscriptions in Ogam.

It may be said in passing that the Ogam character was sometimes used in other material than that of stone, and for purposes widely different from any to which I have hitherto glanced. There exists very strong evidence of its having been applied to wood, and even to iron. Examples occur in bone, amber, gold, silver, and lead. The specimen in lead which I was fortunate enough to discover in 1844, in the possession of an aged Catholic clergyman, who was using the vessel upon which it appeared as an inkbottle, is extremely valuable, not only from the legend being in relief, but also from the circumstance of its discovery in Kilmallock, the name of which place it gives. The Ogams are in two lines, and, if read from the bottom upwards, render the words: *Nig-Lasmeich,* and *Cill Mocholmog.* The object on which they occur is a narrow, quadrangular vessel, one inch and three-eighths in height, with sides converging upwards, and with a low, small circular neck. No doubt, the Ogam character, in one form or another, was not unfrequently used as a charm, or, as shown by Bishop Graves, for purposes of divination.

CHAPTER IV.

GRAVES AND CEMETERIES.

MONUMENT AT HAZLEWOOD — NEWGRANGE — DOWTH — KNOWTH—
SLIEVE-NA-CALLIAGH, NEAR OLDCASTLE, CO. MEATH — MOYTURA —
HEAPSTOWN, CO. SLIGO — THE BARR OF FINTONA — BIGHY, NEAR
FLORENCECOURT, CO. FERMANAGH—DOOHAT, NEAR FLORENCECOURT,
CO. FERMANAGH.

HE extraordinary megalith remaining in
the deer park, Hazlewood demesne, near
Sligo, has for many years proved a sore
puzzle to writers on the subject of Irish lapidary antiquities. It seems impossible to class it with any monument known to British or Irish archæologists, although,
indeed, more than one visionary antiquary has styled
it the "Irish Stonehenge." The structure consists
primarily of an oblong, or blunted oval, figure, formed
of rude, undressed stones, generally of inconsiderable
length and thickness, and averaging but 2 or 3 feet
in height. This central area extends, as nearly as
possible, east and west. Its extreme length is 50 feet
6 inches; its greatest diameter 28 feet. From the
western end extends an oblong compartment, constructed of stones similar to those forming the oval,

measuring 27 feet in length, by 12 feet 6 inches in breadth. The entrance to this extension is by a kind of portal, the sides of which consist of two rude, un-hewn stones, about 3 feet in height. These are sur-mounted by a horizontal lintel, about 8 feet long, and 2 feet 6 inches in thickness. We have thus a perfect trilithon. Fergusson, in his "Rude Stone Monuments," very incorrectly states that these stones, like those forming two similar entrances, to be noticed further on, have been "squared and partially dressed." Most undoubtedly, they have never been touched by hammer or chisel. The western apartment, it should be ob-served, is divided by two projecting stones, which may have been capped with a lintel. The space between them is barely sufficient to allow the passage of a mo-derately-sized man. This end of the monument is composed of two stones of great size, the outermost leaning against its neighbour. They are about 7 feet in length, 2 feet in thickness, and over 6 feet in height. Immediately adjoining, even touching them, to the westward, are the remains of a stone circle, about 20 feet in diameter, the area of which was probably occupied by a low carn or mound. The spot, however, has been so tossed about that little of its pristine character remains.

The same remark applies to the state of a similar circle found at the eastern termination of the monu-ment.

At the eastern extremity of the central enclosure are two projections, precisely similar in style to that which I have described as occurring at the opposite end. They are entered by trilithon opes, the space from ground to lintel measuring about 3 feet. These prolongations, which have been absurdly styled "aisles," run parallel to each other, one measuring 27 feet in length, while its companion, that to the south, is 3 feet shorter. Both are divided into two compartments, of unequal size, by projecting stones. There is a space between them, 5 feet 6 inches broad, but separated from the main oval by an immense block of stone.

"What, then," writes Mr. Fergusson, "is this curious edifice? It can hardly be a tomb: it is so unlike any other tomb which we know of. In plan it looks more like a temple; indeed, it is not unlike the arrangement of some Christian churches; but a church, or temple, with walls pervious, as these are, and so low that the congregation outside can see all that passes inside, is so anomalous an arrangement, that it does not seem admissible. At present it is unique; if some similar example could be discovered, perhaps we might guess its riddle."*

The late E. T. Hardman suggested that it was a place of ceremonial observance of some kind.

It remained for Colonel Wood-Martin, in his learned and exhaustive work on the Rude Stone Monuments of

---

* An almost perfectly similar example occurs in Glen Malin, Co. Donegal. See *Journal* of the Royal Society of Antiquaries of Ireland, for last quarter of 1890. The Glen Malin monument is certainly sepulchral.

Sligo (a volume which should be in the hands of every
student of Irish antiquities) to clear up the mystery in
which the character of this " Irish Stonehenge " was
shrouded. He went to work very vigorously, and
single-handed, his only colleague being a spade. " Excavations," he writes, " made in the four smaller divi-
sions, at the eastern and western extremities of the
monument, clearly demonstrated the fact that they *had
been formerly covered like ordinary kistvaens with roofing
slabs*, as these were found lying in the ground in a
fragmentary state, when the sod was turned up. In
these four excavations human and animal bones were
discovered, all uncalcined. With them was a flint
flake.

" Explorations in the central enclosure were not
attended with equally decisive results; for although in
two instances some traces of osseous remains were
found, yet in other spots the soil appeared to be undisturbed. The conclusion, therefore, may be safely drawn
that the eastern and western 'aisles' are simply uncovered kistvaens; that they were erected when inhuma-
tion burial was practised, and when flint instruments
were in use; but whether the central enclosure had
been used for burial, or merely for ceremonial obser-
vances before committing the bodies to the tomb, could
not be determined with any degree of certainty."

The osseous remains found in various parts of the
monument were submitted to the judgment of several
highly-skilled surgical practitioners, who pronounced
them to be mostly human, and as having belonged to

persons of various ages. Some were evidently those of young children. The bones of the lower animals noticed comprised those of deer, of the horse (apparently), and some of swine. There were also bones of rabbits and hares, as likewise some of birds. All seemed to be strangely mixed together; but the remains in no instance exhibited the action of fire. The flint flake referred to belongs to the class of articles described by Wilde* as approaching in form, but not altogether taking the shape, of a stone celt. "The implement shows traces of careful chipping for a short distance round the segment of a circle which forms its cutting edge, the remainder of the tool being left in a rough unfinished state, with thick blunt sides."

It is probable that the interments are of an extremely early date, but not so early as the time of cremation; and that the animal bones are relics of some grand funeral feast, or feasts.

In the Senchaɼ naɜ Ꞧelec, or "History of the Cemeteries," one of our most ancient manuscripts preserved in the Library of the Royal Irish Academy, we have a list of the regal cemeteries of Erin during a long period prior to the advent of St. Patrick. The late Dr. Petrie, in quoting this tract, observes that—"Judging from its language, its age must be referred to a period several centuries earlier than that in which its transcriber flourished. It is also to be observed that this tract is glossed in its original, especially by Moelmuiri himself,

---

* *Catalogue*, Museum, R. I. A., p. 27.

and that such explanations of the transcriber are given within crotchets, both in the Irish text and the translation of it." Moelmuiri must have made his compilation and transcription at Clonmacnois about A. D. 1100. We are informed in this venerable tract that—

"These were the chief cemeteries before the Faith (*i. e.* before the introduction of Christianity), viz. Cruachan, Brugh, Taillten, Luachair Ailbe, Oenach Ailbe, Oenach Culi, Oenach Colmain, Temhair Erann."*

.   .   .   .

"At Taillten the kings of Ulster were used to bury, viz. Ollamh Fodhla, with his descendants, down to Conchobhar, who wished that he should be carried to a place between Slea and the sea, with his face to the east, on account of the Faith which he had embraced."

From the same authority the two following stanzas are extracted :—

> "The three cemeteries of the idolaters are
> The cemetery of Taillten the select,
> The ever-clean cemetery of Cruachan
> And the cemetery of Brugh."

> "The host of great Meath were buried
> In the middle of the lordly Brugh ;
> The great Ultonians used to bury
> At Taillten with pomp."

The above quotations have been compiled from Petrie's great works on the "Round Towers" and the "Antiquities at Tara Hill." Of the cemeteries named but two can be identified with absolute certainty,

---

* Leabhar na h-Uidhri, p. 51, col. 1.

viz. those of Brugh (now known as Newgrange) upon
the Boyne, and Cruachan, Co. Roscommon; but there is
great probability that Taillten may be the great necro-
polis situate on the Loughcrew Hills not far from
Oldcastle.

Newgrange.—The mausoleum of Newgrange, in
the county of Meath, lying at a distance of about
four miles and a-half of Drogheda, is perhaps, without exception, the most wonderful monument of its
class now existing in any part of western Europe.
In one point, at least, it may challenge comparison
with any Celtic monument known to exist, inasmuch

The Mausoleum of Newgrange, from the east.

as a number of the mighty stones of which its
gallery and chambers, hereafter to be spoken of, are
composed, exhibit a profusion of ornamental design,
consisting of spiral, lozenge, and zig-zag work, such
as is usually found upon the torques, urns, weapons,
and other remains of pagan times in Ireland. We

shall here say nothing of its probable antiquity, as it
is anterior to the age of authentic Irish history ; and
indeed it would be in vain to speculate upon the age of
a work situate upon the banks of the Boyne, which, if
found upon the banks of the Nile, would be styled a
pyramid, and perhaps be considered the oldest of all
the pyramids of Egypt.   The carn (see page 95)

Mouth of the Passage leading to the Great Chamber Newgrange.

which, even in its present ruinous condition, measures
about 70 feet in height, from a little distance
presents the appearance of a grassy hill partially
wooded ; but upon examination the coating of earth is
found to be altogether superficial, and in several places

the stones, of which the hill is entirely composed, are laid bare. A circle of enormous stones, of which eight or ten remain above ground, anciently surrounded its base; and we are informed that upon the summit an obelisk or huge pillar stone, formerly stood. The opening represented at page 96 was accidentally discovered about the year 1699 by labouring men employed in the removal of stones for the repair of a road.

Ornament on the Roof of the Eastern Recess.

It was the external entrance to the gallery, which extends in a direction nearly north and south, and communicates with a chamber or cave nearly in the centre of the mound. This gallery, which measures in length about 50 feet, is, at its entrance from the exterior, 4 feet high; in breadth at the top, 3 feet 2 inches; and at the base, 3 feet 5 inches. These dimensions it retains, except in one or two places where the stones appear to have been forced from their original

position, for a distance of 21 feet from the external
entrance.   Thence towards the interior its size gra-

dually increases, and
its height, where it
forms the chamber, is
18 feet.   Enormous
blocks of stone, ap-
parently water-worn,
and supposed to have
been brought from the
mouth of the Boyne,
form the sides of the
passage ;   and it is
roofed with similar

Ornament on the Roof of the Eastern
Recess.

stones.   The ground plan of the chamber is cruciform,
the head and arms of the cross being formed by three

recesses, one placed di-
rectly fronting the en-
trance, the others east
and west, and each con-
taining a basin of gra-
nite.   The sides of these
recesses are composed of
immense blocks of stone,
several of which bear a
great variety of carving,
supposed by some to be
symbolical.   The engravings represent various characteristic selections from the work upon the roof of the
eastern recess, in the construction and decoration of

Supposed Inscription.

which a great degree of care appears to have been
exercised. An engraving upon a stone forming the
northern external angle of the western recess is supposed to be an inscription; but even could any satisfactory explanation of it be
given, its authenticity is
doubtful, as it has been supposed to have been forged by
one of the many dishonest
Irish antiquaries of the last
century. The same stone,
upon its eastern face, exhibits what appears to have
been intended as a repre-
sentation of a fern or yew
branch. An ornament, or
hieroglyphic, of a similar
character, was found within
an ancient Celtic tomb at
Locmariaker, in Brittany.*
It is a very remarkable fact
that the majority of these
carvings must have been
executed before the stones

Carving on a Stone in the Western
Recess.

upon which they appear had been placed in their
present positions. Of this there is abundant evidence
in the eastern recess, where we find the lines continued over portions of the stones which it would be

* See *Archæologia*, vol. xxv., p. 233.

impossible now to reach with an instrument, and which form the sides of mere interstices.

The following illustrate some decorations of a very peculiar character, which appear upon the sides of the eastern recess.

Carved Stone in Eastern Recess.

Carved Stone in Eastern Recess.

A stone now lying upon the surface of the mound,

a little above ˙the opening already described, is shown in accompanying engraving.

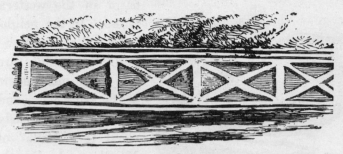

Carved Stone upon the Exterior.

The lower portions of the walls of the chamber are composed of large uncemented stones, placed in an upright position, over which are others laid horizontally, each course projecting slightly beyond that upon which it rests, and so on, until the sides so closely approximate that a single flag suffices to close in and complete the roof, which, in its highest part, is 20 feet above the present level of the floor.

The length of the passage and chamber from north to south is 75, and the breadth of the chamber from east to west, 20 feet. Of the urns or basins contained in the various recesses, that to the east is the most remarkable. It is formed of a block of granite, and appears to have been set upon, or rather within, another of somewhat larger dimensions. Of its form the annexed illustration will give a just idea. Two small circular cavities have been cut within its interior, as represented above, a peculiarity not found in either of the others, which are of much ruder construction, and very shallow. Subjoined is a representation of the

basin in the western recess. In the neighbourhood of the Newgrange tumulus are two other monuments of the same class, and of an extent nearly equal, the " Hills " of Nowth and Dowth, or, as they are called by the Irish, Cnoabh

Stone Basin in the Eastern Recess.

and Dubhath, the former lying about one mile to the westward of Newgrange, and the latter, of which the subjoined is an illustration, at a similar distance in the opposite direction.

Sepulchral Tumulus of Dowth. — Of the internal arrangement of this huge mausoleum, little, until very recently, was known beyond the

Stone Basin in the Western Recess.

fact that it was different from that of the monument last described, inasmuch as, instead of one great gallery leading directly towards the centre of the pile there

appeared here the remains of two passages in a very
ruinous state, and completely stopped up, neither of
which, however, seemed to have conducted towards a
grand central chamber. The Committee of Antiquities
of the Royal Irish Academy having, in the course of the
autumn of 1847, obtained permission from the trustees
of the Netterville Charity, the proprietors of the Dowth

Tumulus of Dowth, from the south.

estate, to explore the interior of the tumulus, the work
was commenced and carried on at considerable cost,
under the immediate direction of Mr. Frith, one of the
county engineers. It should be observed that, from
the difficulty of sinking a shaft among the loose, dry
stones of which this hill, like that of Newgrange, is
entirely composed, Mr. Frith, in order to arrive at the
great central chamber which was supposed to exist,
adopted the plan of making an open cutting from the

base of the mound towards its centre. The first discovery was that of a cruciform chamber upon the
western side, formed of stones of great size, every way
similar to those at Newgrange, and exhibiting the same
style of decoration. A rude sarcophagus, bearing a
striking resemblance to that in the eastern recess at
Newgrange, of which we have given an illustration,
was found in the centre. It had been broken into
several pieces, but the fragments were all recovered
and placed together, so as to afford a perfect idea of
the original form. In clearing away the rubbish with
which the chamber was nearly filled, the workmen
discovered a large quantity of the bones of animals
in a half-burned state, and mixed with small shells. A
pin of bronze and two small knives of iron were also
picked up. With respect to instruments of iron being
found in a monument of so early a date, we may
observe that in the *Annals of Ulster* there occurs a
record of this mound, as well as of several others in the
neighbourhood having been searched by the Northmen
of Dublin as early as A.D. 862 : "On one occasion that
the three kings, Amlaff, Imar, and Ainsle, were plun-
dering the territory of Flann, the son of Coaing;" and
it is an interesting fact that the knives are precisely
similar in every respect to a number discovered, together
with a quantity of other antiques, in the bog of Lagore,
near Dunshaughlin, and which there is reason to refer
to a period between the ninth and the beginning of the
eleventh centuries. Upon the chamber being cleared
out, a passage 27 feet in length was discovered,

the sides of which incline considerably, leading in a westerly direction towards the side of the mound, and composed, like the similar passage at Newgrange, of enormous stones placed edgeways, and covered in with large flags. The chamber, though of inferior

Mouth of Passage leading to the Chamber of Dowth,

size to that of Newgrange, is constructed so nearly upon the same plan, that a description of the one might almost serve for that of the other. The recesses, however, do not contain basins, and a passage extending in a southerly direction, communicating with a series of small crypts, forms here another peculiarity. A huge stone, in height 9 feet, in breadth 8 feet, placed between the northern and eastern recesses, is remarkable

Fig. 1.—Carving on a Stone at Dowth.

for the singular character of its carving (see fig. 1).

A portion of the work upon this stone bears great resemblance to Ogam writing. A sepulchral chamber, of a quadrangular form, portions of which bear a great variety of carving (among which the cross, a symbol which neither in the old nor the *new* world can be considered as pecu-

liar to Christianity, is conspicuous) has been discovered upon the southern side of the mound.

Here, as elsewhere, during the course of excavation, the workmen unearthed vast quantities of bones, half-burned, many of which proved to be human; "several unburned bones of horses, pigs, deer, and birds, portions of the heads of

Fig. 2.—Carving on a Stone at Dowth.

the short-horned variety of the ox, and the head of a fox." They also found a star-shaped amulet of stone, a ring of jet, several beads, and some bones fashioned like pins. Among the stones of the upper portion of the carn were discovered a number of globular balls of stone, the size of small eggs, which Sir W. Wilde supposed probably to have been sling stones. A double circle of stones appears anciently to have surrounded this carn. Of these the greater number lie buried : but in summer-time their position, particularly after a long continuance of sunny weather, is shown by the remarkably dry and withered appearance of the grass above them.

Among the trees between the mound of Dowth and the mansion, are some remains of a small sepulchral chamber; and a little to the east of the house the student will find a grand specimen of the ancient military encampment, or rath.

Since the above account of the grand tumuli of Newgrange and Dowth was written, now forty years ago, scarcely a single change in the internal aspect of the former structure can be perceived. True it is that one of the stones forming the gallery or passage leading to the chamber had slightly slipped inwards, and threatened to block the way. Another stone on the interior had been forced by lateral pressure considerably out of its proper position; and some portion of the neighbouring wall seemed likely to give way for want of its support. However, the attention of the officers of the Board of Public Works, in whose custody the monument is vested, have undertaken to do all that is necessary to strengthen the weaker portions of the structure.

At Dowth, during their work of conservation, carried
out a few years ago, a fine beehive-shaped chamber
was discovered a little to the right of the main gallery.
This should be seen by all students of Irish megalithic
works, especially as it seems perfect in itself, and that
at least one of its side stones exhibits a profusion of
archaic carving kindred to but slightly differing from
anything found at Newgrange.

Tumulus at Knowth.—The other great monument (Knowth) of this group has probably never been
entered since the time it was plundered and doubtlessly
ruined by the Danes.   For many years it has served as
a convenient quarry for builders of houses and repairers
of roads.   That it could be explored at little cost is
certain, as owing to the denudation it has suffered, the
passage or gallery leading to its " cave " has in part
been laid bare.   In any other country such a monument would not for a day be left neglected and a prey
to needy builders and road-contractors.   Its circle, or
circles, are not altogether obliterated, and here and
there some portions remain which show that the work,
though less massive than that of Newgrange, was at
least as striking as anything to be found in Dowth,
or in connexion with the remains at Loughcrew, or
others occurring in the western districts of Ireland.
A visit from Drogheda to Dowth, Newgrange, and
Knowth, could easily be accomplished by car in part
of a summer's day.   The scenery in the district is in
its way perhaps the most beautiful in Ireland.

Pagan Cemetery near Oldcastle, Co. Meath.
—Oldcastle is within an easy railway drive from the
metropolis. There would be no difficulty in visiting
the locality from Dublin, spending a good part of the
day there, and returning in the evening.

To the antiquary—to the explorer of sepulchral remains of a very remote past—the Slieve-na-Calliagh
range of picturesque hills, just over Oldcastle, offers a
quarry almost inexhaustible. There indeed, within the
radius of a rifle-shot, may be seen grouped together the
most extraordinary collection of archaic monuments to
be found in Ireland—perhaps in Western Europe.
These for the most part consist of megalithic sepulchres
surmounted by tumuli, and environed by stone circles.
Many of the stones forming the chambers are covered
with a profusion of carvings, which there is every reason to believe are of a symbolic character. A key to
their meaning, however, has yet to be discovered, if
indeed the mystery in which they are at present enveloped can ever be dispelled. It is, perhaps, not too
much to say that on Sleive-na-Calliagh, and on the
stones at Newgrange and Dowth, may be studied a
greater number of *bizarre* cryptic sepulchral scorings
or devices than to be found in Britain, Caledonia, and
Gaul united.

Not one historical line in connexion with this great
cemetery has been discovered, or at least *absolutely*
identified with it. Until 1858 the very existence of
the antiquities at and around Slieve-na-Calliagh seems
to have been unknown to all but one gentleman,

and a few herds, who believed the carns and other
remains to be the work of a witch named Cailleach
Bhéartha, who, in attempting a wild leap in the adjoining townland of Patrickstown, was unfortunate
enough to fall and break her neck. In August of the
year named I visited the place under the hospitable
guidance of Mr. Searanke, then the worthy County
Surveyor of Meath, an observer possessed of much information on archæological matters, and who had
already noticed and even sketched several of the mysterious carvings which appear upon the stones. On
that occasion I measured and made plans of several of
the remains; and later in the same year drew up a
Paper upon the subject, which Paper was kindly read
in my name, before the Architectural Society of
Oxford, by J. H. Parker, Esq., C. B., the well-
known archæologist of Oxford. I am thus particular
in giving names and dates in connexion with the
first public notice of the antiquities at Slieve-na-Calliagh, as a gentleman, who did not become acquainted
with them until several years after the public reading
of the paper referred to, claimed the honour of being
their " discoverer," a distinction to which he was in
no way entitled.

Nevertheless, the "claimant," the late Eugene
Alfred Conwell, M. R. I. A., &c., Inspector of Irish
National Schools, has done good service to archæology,
inasmuch as, with the liberal co-operation of the late
J. L. W. Naper, D.L., owner of the soil, he has been
enabled to clear out the majority of the chambers,

and investigate what had been left by former searchers
of their contents.   An immense amount of *débris* was
removed, and stones for ages buried brought to light.
Many of the latter are singularly carved, and not a
few present designs not previously known to antiquaries.

The idea seems to have struck Mr. Fergusson, who
at least on one occasion accompanied Mr. Conwell to
the place, that the Loughcrew monuments represented
the once famous, but long-forgotten, cemetery of
Taillten, a place which was supposed to be represented
by the modern Telltown, about fifteen miles distant.
After suggesting many *pros* and *cons* in reference to
the supposed identification, Mr. Fergusson writes :—
" If, however, this is not Taillten, no graves have been
found nearer Telltown which would at all answer to
the description that remains to us of this celebrated
cemetery ; and till they are found, these Loughcrew
mounds seem certainly entitled to the distinction.   I
cannot see that the matter is doubtful."

If this be Taillten, as it very probably is, we may
here study some of the oldest forms of known sepulchral
monuments to be found in Ireland.   According to the
" Annals of the Four Masters," as translated by the
late Dr. O'Donovan, numerous were the kings and
nobles here buried.   The first whose name is mentioned is Ollamh Fodhla, son of Fiacha Finscothach.
Eochaidh was his first name, and " he was called
Ollamh (Fodhla), because he had been first a learned
Ollamh, and afterwards king of Fodhla, *i. e.* of Ire-

land." The Four Masters set down his death as
having occurred in 1277 B.C. Our oldest and most
trustworthy authorities state that Taillten ceased to be
used as a cemetery on the death of Conchobhor, an
Ultonian king, who flourished in Erin at the commencement of the Christian era, and who, according to
the "Annals of Tighernach," died A.D. 33.

The principal monument of the group (the ruins of
about twenty-four, besides numerous smaller graves
remain) measures 116 feet in diameter. It contains a
cruciform chamber, like that at Newgrange, in miniature, the entrance to which faces due east, and is
approached by a shallow, funnel-shaped recess. Round
the base is a closely-set circle of stones, varying from 6
to 12 feet in length, and acting as a kind of retaining
fence to the loose, dry boulders which form the body of
the tumulus. One of these stones has excited peculiar
attention. It is known to the neighbouring people as
the "Hag's Chair." Mr. Fergusson states there can be
little doubt that it was intended as a seat, or throne,
but whether by the king who erected the sepulchre, or
for what purpose, it was difficult to say.

Mr. Conwell, however, was much more sanguine and
precise. Without the slightest authority for so doing
he rushes to the conclusion that this particular mausoleum *must* be the tomb of Ollamh Fodhla, and that the
chair cannot be other than the judicial seat, or throne,
of that famous king. He writes :—" And to whom,
keeping in view the preceding MS. testimony " (the
MSS. only state that the Ollamh was buried at Taillten)

"could this great megalithic chair be more appropriately ascribed than to Ollamh Fodhla? It would be natural to suppose that for the site of the tomb of the great king and law-maker, his posterity (or, indeed, probably he himself, during his own lifetime), selected the most elevated spot on the entire range; hence we propose to call the carn on that spot, 904 feet above the sea-level, and situated on the middle hill, Ollamh Fodhla's tomb; and the great stone seat "Ollamh Fodhla's Chair"; and the ruined remains of the smaller surrounding carns, six of which still remain, the tombs of his sons and grandsons, mentioned in the previous extracts. In fact, on the summit of the highest hill in the site of this ancient royal cemetery, we believe there still exist the remains of the tombs of the dynasty of Ollamh Fodhla"!

A voluminous report of the explorations at Loughcrew, accompanied by a large number of plans and drawings, was prepared by Mr. Conwell, with a view to publication; but the intention, for some reason or other, appears not to have been carried out. A very sketchy account of several of the principal carns, and their scorings, contents, &c., &c., was laid by him before the Royal Irish Academy. This was subsequently printed and circulated, but the materials for the greater work remain neglected, if not forgotten. This is to be regretted; many of the speculations, no doubt, might be well dispensed with, but it is to be presumed the illustrations, especially if from rubbings, and by measured plans, would be of considerable value to archæological inquirers. Such illustrations, however, should be beyond suspicion, and the rubbings not tampered with.

Carns at Moytura and Cong.—There are a considerable number of other great carns, some with stone circles, others plain, distributed over Ireland; but with the exception of those already mentioned there is scarcely one the interior of which has been thoroughly explored. In his "Guide to Lough Corrib," the late Sir William Wilde describes several which are supposed to mark the scene of the battle of Southern Moytura, or Moytirra, fought between the Firbolgs and Tuatha de Danaans, according to the "Annals of the Four Masters," in A. M. 3303. These are, externally, exactly similar to the mounds of Newgrange and Dowth.

Great Monument at Heapstown, Co. Sligo.— At Heapstown, not far from Ballindoon, Co. Sligo, is a gigantic pile of stones, said to have been raised in the fourth century of our era over Oliolla, son of Eochy Moyvane, *ard-righ*, i. e. chief king, of Erin. The extreme circumference of this enormous work, which, by-the-by, the country people assert was erected in one night, is stated to be 62 statute perches. The story of its having had any connexion with Oliolla, is probably as true as that embodied in the peasant's legend. Nothing certain is known of its history, and we are equally ignorant concerning the origin of *Miscan Maeve*, and of the great monuments which seem to have given the name of *Carns* to a townland over Cleveragh, the

beautiful seat of Colonel Wood-Martin. All these are
in the immediate vicinity of Sligo. To mention at
length further instances would be to exceed the limits
of a handbook.

Monument at the Barr of Fintona.—It will
be necessary, however, to notice a few minor typical
and highly interesting sepulchres, some of which it
would appear had been left undisturbed and unnoticed
until the other day. One of the most instructive of
those occurs at the " Barr " of Fintona, about three
miles north of Trillick, Co. Tyrone. My attention had
been drawn to the place by J. G. V. Porter, Esq., owner
of the soil. The carn was found to consist of a mound of
stones, rising to a height of about 8 feet above the then
level of the surrounding bog. It is quite circular in
plan. Resting upon the ground, and just within the
outer edge of the pile, were eight cists, each of
which had the appearance of a small cromleac. Four
of these chambers enclosed portions of the human
skeleton, and in two of them, in addition to the
remains of man, was found a " crock," composed of
baked clay. All within the principal urn-bearing
cavity was perfectly dry and undisturbed. The floor
was flagged, and here and there lay human bones in
various stages of decomposition. With them were
found three vertebræ of a small mammal, probably
those of a dog. A fine, richly-decorated earthen vase
lay on its side in the middle of the enclosure, resting
upon a large clean slab of sandstone. The vessel

evidently reposed as originally deposited. Was it a food vessel, or cup? If it were customary in the so-called "Stone Age" to deposit with human remains a once-prized knife or dagger, arms or ornaments, why should we suppose that the deceased's favourite food-holder or drinking-cup might not have occasionally been left with his remains?

One of the cists lay on the north-east side of the mound. It was oblong in form, 2 feet 4 inches in breadth by 3 feet 6 in length. The sides and bottom were neatly flagged. It was with great toil this grave was reached, as it proved to be secured by *two* ponderous covering stones, one laid immediately over the other. These being at length removed, a sight most startling and indeed impressive was presented. We looked into a chamber or cist which had not seen the light for countless centuries—never since the age of stone! and there upon the floor, cushioned in damp dust, lay the remains, or portions of the skeletons, of two human beings, white and clean, as contrasted with the dark-brown colour of their kindred mould. The crania, which I carefully removed, are now in the Museum, R. I. A. Strange to say, there were no traces of the lower jaws, nor even of teeth. From the narrow proportions of the cist, it is quite manifest that no two perfect human bodies, even those of very young people, could have been there deposited. The space was far too limited to have contained even one unmutilated corpse. The bones exhibited no trace of the action of fire ; they were certainly unburnt, and were unaccom-

panied by traces of charcoal or ashes of any kind.
Upon the mould which lay on the floor being anxiously
sifted no bead, flint-flake, or manufactured article of
any description was discovered; and as the bottom and
sides of the cist were composed of cleanly-split sandstone, it was evident that nothing but human remains
had been there entombed—unless, indeed, we may
suppose that an earthen vessel, or similarly perishable
object had crumbled into dust amongst the animal
matter.

What, then, are we to consider as to the nature of
this deposit? A similar question might arise in connexion with the remains already noticed, as the cists or
graves in which they were found could not possibly
have contained one adult human form, unless the body
had been dissevered *and packed* within the "narrow
house." It is, perhaps, equally singular that while the
crania were fairly perfect, almost the whole of the
remainder of the skeletons should have been mis-
sing.

At a point in the circumference of the mausoleum
which may be described as lying south-east from the
centre was a simple cist of quadrangular form, measuring 17 by 18 in.; its depth was 18 in. The little
chamber was found to contain some traces of grayish
earth, somewhat like lime-mortar; this occurred here
and there in the generally darker mould, and had the
appearance of being a decomposition of human or other
bones. A cavity precisely similar in formation, but
somewhat smaller, lay in the circle, at a distance of

about 9 feet from the cist last noticed. This also
yielded nothing of interest. Upon the north-west side
of the carn were two cists which in my temporary
absence were dug up by treasure-seekers and others.

The havoc here perpetrated by ignorance is greatly
to be lamented, as in one of the cists an ornamental
vase, one fragment of which I was fortunate enough
to recover, had been found. In connexion with
this vessel was discovered a beautifully formed knife
of flint. When perfect, as originally found, it mea-
sured 3 inches and $\frac{3}{10}$ths in length, by $1\frac{1}{2}$ inch at
its broadest part. The blade is extremely thin, and
exhibits on one side a central ridge, the other surface
being flat or slightly convex. Like most implements
of its class, it presents admirably chipped edges.
As a hunter's companion, in the hands of primitive
man, this relic of the so-called " Stone Age " would
have answered several purposes : it would have skinned
the prey, cut or sawn the flesh, and divided the hide of
red deer, wolf, or of almost any animal into the desired
forms for dress or tent-covers ; or into thongs for bow-
strings, slings, or ropes; or for curach manufacture, &c.
The colour was dark gray, and the instrument showed
no evidence of its having been submitted to the action
of fire.

The grave now to be noticed is the last of the group
to which I shall have to refer. It lay nearly midway
between the first described, and the more northern of
the two which had been shattered by the treasure-
seekers. It also was in all but utter ruin, owing

partly to the dampness of its position, and perhaps in some degree to the comparatively inferior material of its component parts. The contents presented human bones—those of adults—so soft and decomposed as not to bear the slightest touch. They suggested the idea of softish mortar, or of putty. No artificial object was here found, though everything was done to bring to light any deposit which might have accompanied the bones.

It is well, perhaps, to state that upon a trench being excavated from the northern side through more than half the diameter of the carn, no central cist, or chamber, was found.

The importance of the discoveries made at the "Barr" in their bearings upon more than one archæological question will doubtlessly, by a careful reader, be acknowledged. Whether the human remains there found, apparently huddled together in cists not sufficiently large to have contained an entire adult body, were those of victims immolated during the celebration of sepulchral rites, or whether they are relics of persons slain in battle, buried, and subsequently disinterred for final sepulture in the territory of their people or ancestors, are questions which it would be very difficult to decide.

Graves at Bighy, near Florencecourt, Co. Fermanagh.—In some respects this is a very remarkable mausoleum. It stands on the lands of Bighy (a modification of the Irish word *Beithigh*,

which signifies Birch-land), on a shoulder of Bennaghlin, a mountain almost overhanging Florencecourt,
the Fermanagh residence of the Earl of Enniskillen,
in a spot which, until lately, was scarcely accessible to
any but the light-limbed herd, or, possibly, to the
adventurous manufacturer of poteen. It is a carn
composed of sandstone, perfectly circular in plan, with
a central chamber, and fifteen or more cists, placed
almost equally distant from each other, and ranged
just within the outer edge of the mound, which measures 50 feet in diameter, and is at present about 10
feet high. The central chamber is of an oval form,
6 feet by 4 feet, and 4 feet in height. It is covered
by two large flagstones and a number of smaller ones.
Its greater axis extends exactly east and west. Of the
surrounding cists, probably eighteen in number, but
three remain in a tolerably fair state of preservation.
The largest of these is of a beehive form, is quite circular, measuring 3 feet 6 inches in diameter. Its
height was probably 4 feet, but, from the disturbed
state of the floor, there is difficulty in taking a very
accurate measurement. Of the other cists, which are
slightly smaller, two presented a rudely quadrangular
plan, and were covered by stones laid horizontally.
With considerable difficulty, owing to the shaky state
of the walls, we diligently searched these cists, finding
in all of them small portions of calcined bones, accompanied by wood charcoal. In the larger and more perfect chamber, situated to the south-west of the mound,
Mr. Gerald Wakeman, who accompanied me, was lucky

enough to find, imbedded amongst a quantity of charcoal and burned bones, the base of a cinerary urn, $2\frac{3}{4}$ inches in diameter. It appears to have been quite plain. No other portion of this vessel was discoverable, and it was quite manifest that this cist, as well as the others in the mound, had been very roughly handled by seekers for the proverbial " crocks of gold," perhaps on many occasions. The carn, it should be noted, was environed by a shallow trench, the edges of which, placed at irregular distances from each other, present a number of rough hillocks, the natural growth of bog-stuff, as we ascertained by digging into several of them.

No doubt, elsewhere in the country carns exhibiting a similar arrangement of cists exist, but the description here given of two representative examples must suffice for the present. Mr. Fergusson does not seem to have been aware of this form of mausoleum, at least as occurring in Ireland.

The star-shaped Monument of Doohat, near Florencecourt, Co. Fermanagh. — Doohat, the land upon which this monument is situate, will be found marked on the Ordnance Map just three and a-half miles, " as the crow flies," due south of Florencecourt. It is two miles from Bighy, on the opposite side of Bennaghlin mountain. It is probably older than history in these countries ; but the name of the site upon which it stands, *Doohat* (ꝺumhᴀ ᴀιᴄ), " *the place of the sepulchral tumulus*," sufficiently explains that at one time its character had not passed out of local recollection.

The plan of the work is, as far as I know, unique in Ireland, representing a star-fish, with five rays projecting from a central body or chamber of the usual "giant's grave" class. To the south of the chamber, and apparently forming a portion of the original design, occurs a semicircular ridge of stones. This feature is constructed in the same manner as the rays, and differs from them only in form and want of connexion with any other portion of the carn. To a fanciful mind the plan, on the whole, would most readily suggest the idea of a star and crescent. Whether the design had anything to do with religious symbolism of any kind, it is not for me to say. All that need be here stated is that the rays are well-defined, stony ridges, averaging 16 or 17 feet in breadth at their junction with the central cist, or dolmen, from which point they taper off to distances of 60, 46, 42, and 40 feet respectively. They terminate very sharply with one, or two, or three stones. The largest terminal stone, that which finishes the north-western ray, measures 3 feet 6 inches by 2 feet.

The main chamber, which extends north and south, is divided by stone partitions into three compartments, of which the central one, measuring 8 feet by 4 feet internally, is the largest. From its north-western angle a rudely quadrangular offset, about 3 feet on the sides, projects westwards. This tomb differs in no respect from a number of giants' graves or dolmens which are found in various parts of the country. No trace of covering slabs, if any such were ever used to overlap the chamber, can be discovered within or without the quadrangles, and it is not in the least likely that any considerable portion of the work has been removed. There is an over-abundance of stones, large and small, in the immediate neighbourhood ready at hand, and there are no buildings near which could have been furnished with materials from this source. Into this chamber we carefully excavated down to the "till," or undisturbed yellow clay, without finding any relics of the past beyond small pieces of wood charcoal, stones showing the action of fire, very dark-coloured, unctuous earth, and here and there some grayish matter, which may have been bone in the last stage of decomposition. Having religiously refilled all the pits necessarily made during our search, even replacing the rubbish which had fallen or been thrown into the chambers, we left the work in the same condition as that in which we had found it.

We then proceeded to examine a number of small cists, some fifteen in all, which are situate in the various rays. Most of these diminutive receptacles had evidently been previously searched. Of the six into which we introduced the spade four presented small pieces of calcined bone, burned earth and stones, black, greasy clay, and considerable quantities of charcoal. There was much osseous sediment, resembling gray turf ashes well moistened with water. The cists had, doubtlessly, all been originally covered by flags, and would have presented the appearance of miniature dolmens. In design they were irregularly circular,

composed of five or more small stones, which in a manner lined the mouth of a little pit sunk about a foot or
so into the "till." The dimensions of the largest, and
I may say perfect, cist are as follows :—2 feet 2 inches
by 2 feet 3 inches ; depth, as well as could be ascertained, 2 feet. That they had ever contained urns is
highly improbable, as not a fragment of pottery
appeared to reward our search.

"Horned cairns," bearing a general likeness to the
Doohat monument, are not uncommon in Scandinavia.
They are also found in the north of Scotland. Tri-
angular-shaped graves were generally supposed to be
confined to Scandinavia, but at least one example, as
noticed by Colonel Wood-Martin, occurs in Ireland.
See the chapter on Moytirra, in "Rude Stone Monuments of Sligo."

Mounds. — Mounds of earth, occasionally mixed
with stones, were sometimes erected as places of interment by an early people in Ireland. They partake
very much of the character of carns, from which class
of sepulchre they may be said to differ only in material,
the carns being entirely of stone. Some interesting
examples may be seen in the immediate vicinity of
Dublin, at and beyond the village of Clontarf. These
have been usually, but I believe without warrant, associated with the great battle fought on Good Friday,
1014, in which Brian, the son of Kennedy, commonly
called *Brian Boroimhe*, or "of the Tributes," fell, in
the arms of Victory. The mounds are certainly not

Scandinavian, as in one of them at least, an ordinary
Celtic sepulchral urn, now in the museum of Canon
Grainger, Broughshane, Co. Antrim, was found.
Further, in the tumulus near "Conquer Hill," evidently one of this series, lying at a little distance
nearer Howth, it was remembered by Petrie that a
bronze sword, as well as other relics composed of that
material, occurred. Bronze weapons were certainly
not used either by the Irish or Northmen in Ireland
so late as the eleventh century.

CHAPTER V.

STONE CIRCLES AND ALIGNMENTS.

CIRCLES AT SLIEVE-NA-GREIDLE; AT NEWTOWNBUTLER, CO. FERMA-
NAGH; AT NEWGRANGE; AND ELSEWHERE—ALIGNMENTS.

TONE circles of great magnitude are to be seen in many parts of Ireland. Of the lesser kind numerous examples occur in various counties, and particularly in the north and north-west. They are invariably composed of rough, un-hewn blocks, varying in height from 2 to 11 feet or more above the level of the adjoining land; and in some instances are encompassed with a low, earthen mound or ditch. Their area, though often apparently unoccupied, is not unfrequently found to contain some or other of the following remains :—

1. A cromleac; as at the "Broadstone," parish of Finvoy, Co. Antrim, and scores of other places.
2. A tumulus, or carn ; as at Newgrange, Dowth, Knowth, and elsewhere.
3. A smaller circle, or circles.
4. Menhirs, or pillar stones.
5. Cists.

Human bones, cinerary urns, ashes ; weapons, implements, or ornaments of bone or flint, &c., &c., are almost invariably discovered within these enclosures upon the earth being disturbed.

The urns are usually enclosed between four stones, covered by a flag, and are rarely found at a greater depth from the surface than about 1 foot or 18 inches.

Slieve-na-Greidle Circle.—One of the most interesting circles (for reasons hereafter to be stated),

Stone Circle at Slieve na-Greidle, Co. Down.

occurs on Slieve-na-Greidle, or Griddle Mountain, near Downpatrick, in the county of Down; but several of much greater magnitude claim our attention at present.

Circle near Newtownbutler, Co. Fermanagh. —Probably the most notable circle now remaining in Ireland is that called the "Druid's Temple," situate on the summit of a hill near Wattle Bridge, a small hamlet in the vicinity of Newtownbutler, Co. Fermanagh. Not the slightest notice of this structure has, as far as I am aware, been hitherto published, nor have any drawings of it appeared. It seems to have been wholly unknown to Mr. Fergusson. The stones vary in length from 3 to upwards of 10 feet. The largest remaining measures slightly over 10 feet; it is 6 feet 5 inches in breadth, and 3 feet 9 inches in thickness. Another is 7 feet high, 8 feet 5 inches broad, and 5 feet in thickness. The circle on the interior measures in diameter 126 feet. The diameter of the outer ring at Stonehenge is generally stated (according to Fergusson), to be 100 feet.

Whether this circle was ever enclosed by an outer work, as was common with kindred structures in Britain and elsewhere, can probably never be ascertained. For more than two hundred years the land immediately adjoining has been subject to the plough. That there were outside works, however, can scarcely admit of a doubt. On the south-east side, at a distance of five paces from the circle, are five large stones, the ruins of a dolmen which many years ago, in the memory of a person recently dead at the time of my visit, had been wrecked for the sake of its material. My informant was Mr. John Mackey, postmaster of the neighbouring village. He stated that his father, who had died just five years before, at the age of ninety, used to tell how he had witnessed the destruction of the dolmen or cromleac. The old gentleman used further to affirm that

before the " rooting up " of the place, the ground for
a considerable space round the megalith was regularly
paved with flagstones.   Surely Lord Erne, who resides
close to the spot, and is, I believe, owner of the soil,
might well investigate the character, in all its details,
of this unique monument.

Circle at Newgrange.—The stones which encompass the monuments of Newgrange and Dowth are

Circle at Newgrange.

generally very large, some of them measuring 8 or 9
foot in height.   The engraving represents a portion of
the circle at the former place, of which a description
has already been given.   There are several minor
examples in the same neighbourhood, but they are
in a great state of dilapidation, and, with one exception, would hardly repay a student for the time
occupied in visiting them, particularly as the grander
remains at Newgrange are so accessible.   I may state,

however, that portions of a fine circle, or rather oval, lie a little to the east of Dowth Hall, to the left of the road from Drogheda. Many of the stones have been removed, but several of gigantic proportions remain in their ancient position.

Remains of a Circle near Dowth.

Some of the finest monuments of the class under notice which I have seen in Ireland occur near the shore of Lough Gur, at a short distance to the north of the little town of Bruff, in the county of Limerick, and in the immediate vicinity of Raphoe, in the north-west respectively.

For the purposes of a handbook, however, a sufficient number of typical examples have already been given. A circle, encompassing a cromleac, formerly stood upon Dalkey Common, but it has disappeared, the stones having been blasted and quarried by some public contractor engaged in the erection of the Martello Tower near that place. This outrage occurred about the beginning of the present century, when Dalkey Common was almost a desert. Since then hundreds of houses, walls, &c., &c., have been built upon the Common with the stone of the district, which is yet so abundant that material for the erection of a city might be removed and hardly missed.

Alignments.—In many parts of France, England, and Scotland may be seen lines of stones placed upon end, and generally some few feet apart. The row is occasionally of a length not exceeding a few yards; but sometimes it appears to cover ground which might be measured by miles. The size of the stones in each group is extremely various, some of the blocks being of large proportions, and others measuring barely three or four feet in height. All are invariably untouched, by a tool, presenting the appearance of rough surface stones, or of such as are usually found in glacial-scooped ravines, or river beds. These lines are never single, and usually present parallel rows, varying in number from four or five to ten or more. For want of a better name, these relics of a mysterious past have been variously styled avenues, alignments, rows, parallelitha, &c., &c. It is not too much to assert that works of the kind, even from the days of Stukeley, have presented the most difficult problem which it has been the task of many British and foreign antiquaries to solve. Hitherto we have had little beyond conjecture referring to their uses. They seem like "galleries which lead to nothing." Tombs, temples, or processional avenues they could not have been; yet their construction affords unmistakable evidence of organized labour and deliberate design.

Of remains of this class but two have hitherto been recognized in Ireland. In point of magnitude our alignments, if I may use the term, cannot be compared with those of France or England; but they may not be unfavourably compared with some described by Sir Henry Dryden as seen by him in Scotland. It is, perhaps, well here to observe, that in not a few instances in Ireland we possess lines of stones, sometimes single—never more than dual—which, however, should not be confounded with those of the alignment class, as they are undoubtedly the remains of passages which led to sepulchral chambers, and have been either stripped of their covering slabs, or were never finished. Such rows may indeed sometimes be looked upon as portions of ruined dolmens, or skeleton traces of monuments like those of the Boyne, or like that of Maes-Howe in Orkney. We find such stones of various sizes, differing, as at Finner, near Ballyshannon, from $1\frac{1}{2}$ to 2, or 2 feet 6 inches, or so, above ground; or as at Breagho and Killee, near Enniskillen, with an elevation of 6 or 7 feet. No definite opinion can be formed as to what kind of monument the two latter groups of stones should be assigned, though they in all probability represent but wrecks of works of a sepulchral class, which at a time now forgotten, but almost certainly modern, were exhumed during the process of turf-cutting. Of these, as well as several other broken or never-completed relics of a megalithic class, found in several parts of Ireland, it is only certain that they rest on the "till" upon which peat, to a depth of from 8 to 12 feet, or more, once lay. Many of the mountain, or at least highland, levels of the northern portions of the British Islands, appear to have been gradually enveloped in bog to an extent which, if based on usually-received scientific calculations concerning the average rate of the growth of peat, would give works of human construction found upon the supporting clay an age of at least 4000 years.

The antiquities of Cavancarragh, a district situate on a shoulder of Toppid Mountain, about four miles from Enniskillen, consist of two chambered carns, a stone circle, and a small but well-defined alignment. The latter, and the circle, within the memory of persons still vigorous, lay buried to a depth of from 8 to 12 feet beneath the surface of a mountain bog. The alignment, consists of rows of stones, four in number, extending, as far as can be traced, 480 feet in a direction very slightly N. W. and S. E. The blocks average about 3 feet in height by 2 feet in width, and 6 inches in thickness, and present the appearance of the ordinary red sandstone flags of the district. The extreme south-eastern portion of the work has probably been destroyed ; but in that direction the lines could never have extended much further than they do at present, as the ground suddenly descends, forming one side of a deep ravine, through which in winter time a mountain torrent usually rushes, still carrying on the sculpturings of Nature. How far to the N. W. the lines may be traced is at present uncertain, and cannot be known until the peat in that direction shall have been further

lowered. Probably, however, beyond the circle no considerable extension would be discovered. The carns
here are in a very ruinous condition, having for the
greater part of a century served as a quarry for
building purposes. The plan of one of them is
extremely similar to that of the monument at the
"Barr" of Fintona already described. There was
no central chamber. Only two of its circle of cists
remain in a good state of preservation. The stone
circle standing near the N. W. side of the avenue is
20 feet in diameter, and is formed of twelve sandstone blocks which at present rise but 2 or 3 feet
above the level of the bog.

A second alignment extends to a distance of about
40 feet in a north-easterly direction from the circle
upon Slieve-na-Greidle, or Griddle Mountain, near
Downpatrick, Co. Down. It is composed of stones of
large size, but considerably smaller than those of the
circle.

CHAPTER VI.

RATHS AND DUNS—THE LIS OR CATHAIR—THE CASHEL —SUBTERRANEAN CHAMBERS.

RATH OF DOWNPATRICK — SUBTERRANEAN CHAMBERS — HILL OF TARA—RATH GRAINE—RATH CAELCHU—THE BANQUETING HALL— THE LIS OR CATHAIR—THE CASHEL—STAIGUE FORT—DUN AENGHUIS.

THE earthen duns, or raths, which are found in every part of Ireland where stone is not abundant, often consist merely of a circular entrenchment, the area of which is slightly raised above the level of the adjoining land. But they most frequently present a steep mound, flat at the top, and strongly entrenched, the works usually enclosing a space of ground upon which, it is presumed, the houses of lesser importance anciently stood, the mound being occupied by the dwelling of the chief. The annexed engraving represents the celebrated rath at Downpatrick, in the county of Down, formerly called Rath Keltair, or, sometimes, *Dundalethglas,* or the "fort of the two broken fetters," and will afford an excellent idea of the general appearance of the more remarkable of these remains.

Of the number of raths which I have examined not
one was found to contain a chamber in the mound;
but when the work consists simply of the circular enclosure, of which mention has been already made, excavations of a bee-hive form, lined with uncemented
stones, and connected by passages sufficiently large to
admit a man, are not unfrequently found. These
chambers were probably used as places of temporary

Rath of Downpatrick.

retreat, or as storehouses for perishable commodities,
the want of ventilation, save that derived from the
narrow external entrance, rendering them unfit for the
continued habitation of man. I am not aware that
any rath in the immediate neighbourhood of Dublin
contains a chamber or chambers of this kind. They
are common only in the southern and western parts of
Ireland ; but subterranean works, similar to those
usually found in the forts of Connaught or Munster,
occur in Meath and Louth, and perhaps in other
Leinster counties. An excavation which, some forty

years ago, was accidentally discovered upon the grounds of P. P. Metge, Esq., in the vicinity of Navan, may be described as a good example.

The chamber A is of an oval form, and measures in length 11, in height 6, and in breadth 9 feet; B is a passage or gallery (in length 15 feet), which has fallen in at c; D D are niches let into the sides of the gallery, which, like the chamber, is lined with uncemented stones, laid pretty regularly.

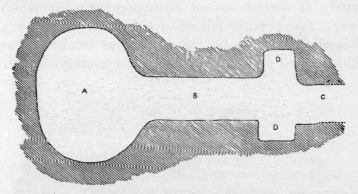

Plan of a Subterranean Chamber near Navan.

The celebrated Hill of Tara, in the county of Meath, from the earliest period of which we have even traditional history, down to the middle of the sixth century, appears to have been a chief seat of the Irish kings. Shortly after the death of Dermot, the son of Fergus, in the year 563, the place was deserted, in consequence, it is said, of a curse pronounced by St. Ruadan, or Rodanus of Lorha, against that king and his palace. After thirteen centuries of ruin, the chief monuments

for which the hill was at any time remarkable are
distinctly to be traced. They consist, for the most
part, of circular or oval enclosures and mounds, called,
in Irish, *Raths* and *Duns*, within or upon which the
principal habitations of the ancient city undoubtedly
stood. The names by which the various remains are
here described are given altogether on the authority of
the Ordnance Survey Map, upon which they were laid
down by Petrie and O'Donovan, after a very careful
study of several ancient Irish documents, in which
were found most minute descriptions, occasionally
accompanied by plans, of the various monuments as
they existed previously to the twelfth century.

The Forradh.

The rath called *Rath Righ*, or *Cathair Crofinn*, appears
anciently to have been the most important work upon
the hill, but it is now nearly levelled to the ground.
This rath, which is of an oval form, measures in length
from north to south about 850 feet, and appears in
part to have been constructed of stone. Within its

enclosure are the ruins of the *Forradh*, a mound of which the preceding engraving is an accurate representation, and of *Teach Cormac*, or the house of Cormac. The mound of the Forradh is of considerable height, flat on the top, and encircled by two lines of earth having a ditch between them. Set in its centre, as already stated in my notice of menhirs or dallans, is a very remarkable pillar stone, supposed to be the Lia Fail, or Stone of Destiny.

A small mound called *Dumha-na-n-Gaill*, or the Mound of the Hostages, is a characteristic example of its class.

The *Teach Cormac*, lying to the south-east of the *Forradh*, with which it is joined by a common parapet, may be described as a double enclosure, the rings of which upon the western side become connected. Its diameter is about 140 feet.

An inspection of these remains alone will afford the student of Irish antiquities a very correct idea of the general character of the ordinary raths or duns; but as I shall suppose the reader to be upon the spot, he is strongly recommended to examine the three great raths called *Rath Graine*, *Rath Caelchu*, and *Fothath Rathagraine*, respectively. Rath Graine is recorded to have belonged to, and to have been named after, Graine, a daughter of King Cormac Mac Art, and wife of Finn Mac Cumhaill, the Fingal of Macpherson's "Ossian."

The ruins of *Teach Midhchuarta*, or the Banqueting Hall of Tara, occupying a position a little to the northeast of *Rath Righ*, consists of two parallel lines of earth, running in a direction nearly north and south, and divided at intervals by openings which indicate the position of the ancient doorways. Their entrances appear to have been twelve in number (six on each side ; but as the end walls, which are now nearly level with the ground, may have been pierced in a similar way, it is uncertain whether this far-famed *Teach Midhchuarta* had anciently twelve or fourteen entrances. Its interior dimensions, 360 by 40 feet, indicate that it was not constructed for the accommodation of a few ; and that the songs of the old Irish bards, descriptive of the royal feasts of *Teamor*, may not be the fictions that many people are ready to suppose them to be. If, upon viewing the remains of this ancient seat of royalty, we feel disappointed, and even question the tales of its former magnificence, let us consider that since the latest period during which the kings and chiefs of Erin were wont here to assemble, thirteen centuries have elapsed, and our surprise will not be that so few indications of ancient grandeur are to be found, but that any vestige remains to point out its site.

The Lis, or Cathair.—In order to afford the reader a clear insight into the character of Irish antiquities generally, it will be necessary to describe a class of ruins now remaining, chiefly in the more remote districts of Connaught and Munster.   I allude to the stone *Cathair*, or, as it is sometimes styled, *Lis, Casieal,* or *Dun,* which is found so commonly along the western and south-western coasts of Ireland, and upon the adjoining islands.   They probably owe their preservation to the abundance of stone in the districts where they are generally found, the neighbouring inhabitants thus having no inducement to destroy them for the sake of their materials.

The subjoined engraving represents a model, which may be seen in the Museum of the Royal Dublin Society's House, of the Cathair at Staigne, in the

Model of Staigue Fort, or Cathair, Co. Kerry.

county of Kerry, probably the most perfect example of its class to be met with in any part of the south of Ireland.   It consists of a circular wall of uncemented stones, about 18 feet in height and 12 in thickness, enclosing an area of 88 yards in diameter.   Upon the internal surface of the wall are regular flights of steps —the plan of which will be best understood by a reference to the woodcut—leading to the highest part of the building.   The doorway is composed of large unhewn stones, and is covered by a horizontal lintel. A ditch, now nearly filled up, anciently defended the wall upon the exterior.

The fortress called *Dun Aenghuis,* upon the great

island of Aran, in the bay of Galway, originally
consisted of four barriers of uncemented stones, the
space between the walls, varying between 640 and 28
feet, defended upon the exterior by a kind of *chevaux-
de-frise*, formed of large and jagged masses of limestone, set in the clefts of the rock upon which the fort
stands. The inner barrier, which in some parts is 10
feet in thickness and 12 feet in height, and which in its
thickness contains a chamber capable of containing but
two or three persons, is composed of three distinct
walls of irregular masonry, lying close together, and
apparently forming one mass. Upon the internal face
of this triple wall are ranges of steps similar to those
in Staigue fort. The external division rises several
feet higher than the other portion, and forms a kind of
breastwork, well adapted to cover the defenders of the
fort from the missiles of assailants.

Several cathairs are not circular in plan, but appear
to have been formed to suit the contour of the eminence
upon which they stand ; and others are of an oval form.
Small circular stone-roofed buildings, called *Clochans*,
are commonly found within their enclosure ; and similar
structures, unconnected with any other work, are numerous in the counties of Galway and Kerry. Upon
High Island, off the coast of Connemara ; Inis Glory,
off the coast of Erris ; and upon other islands adjoining
the western and south-western coasts of Ireland, are
houses built upon precisely the same plan, which were
evidently erected in connexion with ancient monastic
establishments.

PART II.

𝕰𝖆𝖗𝖑𝖞 𝕮𝖍𝖗𝖎𝖘𝖙𝖎𝖆𝖓 𝕬𝖓𝖙𝖎𝖖𝖚𝖎𝖙𝖎𝖊𝖘.

———◆◇◆———

INTRODUCTORY.

ONG had it been considered as an established
fact that the churches of Ireland, previously
to the twelfth century, were altogether constructed of wood, or wattles daubed with
clay, and that consequently there remained
in the country not a single example of church architecture of a period much antecedent to A. D. 1148, in which
year died Malachy O'Morgair, who is stated to have
erected the first ecclesiastical building of stone which
had ever appeared in Ireland. The well-directed labours
of one true antiquary, who, leaving the beaten track of
what was miscalled investigation, sought among our
antiquities themselves for evidences by which their era
might be determined, and in our hitherto neglected
manuscripts, for notices relative to such structures as
were in use at the time of their composition—have
lately shown how little a question, so interesting to

every lover of Ireland, was understood even by the
most judicious writers of the many who had dwelt
upon the subject.

With Dr. Petrie, indeed, rests the honour of having
removed the veil of obscurity which had so long
shrouded the subject of our ecclesiastical antiquities,
and to have shown that Ireland not only contains
examples of church architecture of the earliest period
of Christianity in the kingdom, but also that they
exhibit many characteristics of unrivalled interest.
Following Dr. Petrie on a subject which he has
taken so much time and thought to elucidate, I could
not hope to bring forward much new matter; but even
were it in my power to do so, the scope of this volume
would preclude more than a general sketch. I shall
treat the subject broadly, pointing out the more striking features of what may with justice be styled our
national ecclesiastical architecture, but leaving its
more minute though not less interesting details for
the future study of any who may wish to pursue the
inquiry.

CHAPTER I.

ORATORIES.

EXAMPLES IN KERRY—THEIR SINGULAR CONSTRUCTION—CLOCH-
AWNS, OR BEE-HIVE HOUSES—ORATORY AND BEE-HIVE HOUSE ON
BISHOP'S ISLAND, KILKEE—ST. FECHIN'S MONASTERY ON HIGH
ISLAND, CO. GALWAY—ST. MOLAISE'S ESTABLISHMENT ON INIS-
MURRAY, CO. SLIGO—DEVENISH ISLAND, LOUGH ERNE.

ISLANDS lying off the coast of Ireland, or washed by inland lake or river, are frequently rich in primitive ecclesiastical remains. Before describing the style of church usually found in connexion with our most ancient establishments, whether upon island or mainland, it will be well to devote a chapter to those very remarkable oratories, which, though few in number, form among the early structures of Ireland a most interesting and important class.

Dr. Petrie, in his work entitled "An Inquiry into the Origin and Uses of the Round Towers of Ireland," has described and engraved one of the most beautifully constructed and perfectly preserved of those ancient edifices now remaining. It stands near Smerwick Harbour, in the county of Kerry, and measures externally 43 feet in length by 10 feet in breadth ; its height to the apex of the roof is 16 feet. The building is

composed altogether of uncemented stones, well fitted
to each other, and is roofed by the gradual approximation of the side walls from their base upwards. A
square-headed doorway, placed in the centre of the
west gable, measures in height 5 feet 7 inches; in
breadth at the lintel 1 foot 9 inches; and at the base
2 feet 4 inches. The walls are 4 feet in thickness at
the base. The eastern gable contains a small semicir-
cularly-headed window, the arch being cut out of two

Bee-hive House on Bishop's Island, near Kilkee.

stones. In connexion with the greater number of
these remains are to be seen the ruins of small circular
structures, which appear to have been the habitations
of the ancient ecclesiastics. A fine and hitherto
unnoticed example occurs upon the rock called Bishop's
Island, near Kilkee, upon the coast of Clare. It measures in circumference 115 feet; the exterior face of
the wall, at four different heights, recedes to the depth
of about 1 foot, a peculiarity not found in any other
structure of the kind, and which was probably intro-

duced with the view of lessening the weight of the dome-shaped roof, which was formed, not on the principle of the arch, but, as usual, by the gradual approximation of the stones as the wall ascended. The erection of the oratory adjoining is traditionally ascribed to St. Senan, who lived in the sixth century, and whose chief establishment was upon Inis Cathaigh, or Scattery Island, the Iona of the more southern part of Ireland.

St. Senan's Oratory on Bishop's Island, near Kilkee.

It measures 18 feet by 12 ; the walls are in thickness 2 feet 7 inches ; the doorway, which occupies an unusual position, in the south side, immediately adjoining the west-end wall, is 6 feet in height ; 1 foot 10 inches wide at the top ; and 2 feet 4 inches at the bottom ; the east window spays externally, and in this respect is probably unique in Ireland. Several large monumental pillar stones stand at a short distance from the church, in an easterly direction, but they bear no inscriptions or symbols. The ancient recluses, or anchorites, appear to have selected the wildest and most dreary spots as their places of abode. Bishop's Island, or, as it is styled in Irish, *Oileán-an-Easpoiggortaigh*," i. e. the "island of the hungry or starving bishop," is a barren precipitous rock, environed with perpendicular or over-hanging cliffs, about 250 feet in height. It contains about three quarters of an acre of surface, to which access is most difficult, and only to be effected by a skilful climber, and after a long continuance of calm weather. The island of *Ard-Oileán,* or High Island, off the coast of Connemara, upon which are several of these circular habitations, and a church erected by Saint Fechin in the seventh century, are perhaps equally diffi-cult of access. The ruins are encompassed by a wall, *caiseal,* or *cashel,* of uncemented stones, and occupy a position near the centre of the island. Sheep, which in summer are sent hither from the mainland to graze upon the short sweet grass with which a great portion of the island is covered, and a few martins, are their only occupants. Indeed, such is the lonely and desolate character of the place, that even the very birds appear in some measure to have lost their instinctive dread of intruders; and at the time of our visit, in the summer of 1839, the ground was literally strewn with their eggs, laid upon a few twigs of heath, or upon withered grass or straw, which had been probably picked up from the surface of the sea.

But of all the places in Ireland which should be visited by the student of early Irish ecclesiastical anti-quities, the Island of Inismurray, lying off the coast of Sligo, and generally readily accessible from the town of Sligo, or from Streedagh Point near Grange, is the most important and instructive.

Inismurray.—I am kindly permitted by Richard Jones, Esq., of Streedagh House, Grange, near Sligo, to state for the information of intending pilgrims to Inismurray that upon receiving some days' notice of their intention to visit the place, he could arrange with certain native fishermen to have a proper craft in waiting at Streedagh Point. The cost of the trip to and fro would be from one pound to thirty shillings, according to the number to be conveyed or the state of the weather. The distance from the Point is about four miles or so, and the sail or row on a fine day may be accomplished in little over an hour. Colonel Wood-Martin states that "Tourists can be conveyed in a good five-ton boat from Rosses Point, near Sligo, for thirty shillings; and that, if the wind be favourable, this is the pleasanter, as well as the shorter route."

The *Martyrology of Donegal* presents the following notice of the founder of this establishment :—

"August 12th, Molaisse, *i.e.* Laisrén, son of Deglan, of Inis Muiredaich, in the north (*i.e.* the north of Connaught); he it was who at the cross of Ath-Imlaisi pronounced sentence of banishment on St. Columba."

I need hardly state that these saints flourished in the sixth century, and that the latter-named was no other than the great apostle of the Picts, whose principal foundation in Scotland was Iona.

The following list of the antiquities remaining upon Inismurray I reproduce from my notice of that Island published in the "Journal of the Royal Historical and Archæological Association of Ireland" for October, 1885, No. 64 :—

1. The *Cashel*, or Stone Fort, with its *cellæ*.
2. *Teach Molaise*, the Oratory or Dwelling of St. Molaise.
3. *Teampull-na-Bfear*, or the "Church of the Men." This was, no doubt, the *Teampull Mór*, or great church of the establishment. It is sometimes styled the "Monastery"; and is also known as *Teampull Molaise*.
4. *Teampull-na-Teinidh*, or the "Church of the Fire." This structure is evidently less ancient than the other ecclesiastical buildings remaining upon the island.
5. *Teampull-na-Mban*, or the "Church of the Women."
6. A number of altars, within and without the cashel, most of them bearing very ancient and curiously carved crosses of stone, swearing stones, &c., &c.
7. Two monuments of a class usually styled "Hole-stones," which are held in high veneration on account of certain supernatural powers which they are supposed to possess.
8. Eight memorial *Leacs*, bearing inscriptions in Irish or Latin.
9. Monumental stones, unlettered, but bearing inscribed crosses of extremely early form.
10. Several *Bullàns*, or font-like objects of stone, the precise use of which has not yet been ascertained.
11. Sacred Wells, with their coverings of stone.
12. *Leachta*, or Stations.
13. *Teach-an-Alis*, or the Sweat House.

The above catalogue comprises every class of remain to be found on this singularly interesting Island, which may in a manner be described as a museum of antiquities relating chiefly to the earlier period of the ancient Irish Church. To the wells and some of the monuments I shall have to refer further on.

Devenish Island.—Archæological students, or tourists in quest of the picturesque, who may visit the North of Ireland, and chance to be in the neighbourhood of Enniskillen, should by all means see the famous Island of Devenish, lying in Lough Erne, at a distance of about two miles from the town. Rowboats and men to pull them can be easily engaged at a very moderate cost—if a bargain be made before starting. The patron of this Island bore the name Molaise. Dr. Reeves, Bishop of Down, Connor, and Dromore, has taken care to point out that St. Molaise, or Laisrén, of Inismurray is not to be confounded with St. Molaisi Diamhinsi, or Devenish, son of Nadfraoich, whose day is the 12th September.

Here we find the walls of the oratory of the saint; they are truly Cyclopean in style. Not far distant stands the model Round Tower of Ireland in a state of perfect preservation. In one respect its cornice is unique, inasmuch as it displays an array of rich mouldings in the Hiberno-Romanesque character, and four human heads supposed to represent SS. Patrick, Brigid, Columba, and Molaise, respectively.

CHAPTER II.

CHURCHES.

EARLY CHURCHES—THEIR CHARACTERISTICS—EXAMPLES AT KIL-
LINEY, DALKEY, AND KILTERNAN, COUNTY OF DUBLIN—THE SEVEN
CHURCHES OF GLENDALOUGH, COUNTY OF WICKLOW—ST. KEVIN'S
BED—ST. COLUMBA'S HOUSE AT KELLS, COUNTY OF MEATH.

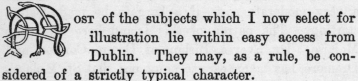 OST of the subjects which I now select for illustration lie within easy access from Dublin. They may, as a rule, be considered of a strictly typical character.

Incredible as it may appear to those who have paid but slight attention to the subject of the ancient ecclesiastical antiquities of Ireland, it is nevertheless a fact that there exist in this country some hundreds of churches, which, in point of antiquity at least, may be classed amongst the most remarkable structures of Christian times now to be found in Europe. The remains of which we shall speak carry with them incontestable evidence of their remote era. Their architectural features and details are of such a character that the surprise is not so great on account of their antiquity in *Christian* "Teampulls," as at their appearance in structures of an era so comparatively late, for they are often truly Etruscan.

Of their usual characteristics we shall here give a

brief description, referring the reader who may desire more than a general sketch to Dr. Petrie's beautiful work already mentioned, in which the subject has been fully discussed.

1. *Doorways.* — Covered by a horizontal lintel, or headed with a semicircular arch, springing from plain, square-edged imposts. Occasionally the arch is cut out of a single stone. At Glendalough are examples in which the lintel is surmounted by a semicircular arch, the space between being filled up with masonry. The stones generally extend the whole thickness of the wall. Few of the very early doorways exhibit any kind of decoration beyond a plain projecting band, of which there are some fine examples at Glendalough. The door appears to have been placed against the interior face of the wall, as in many instances the stones, for a distance of about three inches from the angle, have been slightly hollowed, evidently for the reception of a frame.

2. *Windows.* — Invariably small, and, with one or two exceptions, splaying internally; headed, generally, with small semicircular arches, either formed of several small stones, or cut out of a single large one; but the horizontal lintel is common, as is also a triangular head. The sides of the windows, like the doorway jambs, almost invariably incline. They are rarely decorated, and then in the simplest manner, by a projecting band, similar to that occasionally found upon the early doorways, or by a small bead.

3. *Choir Arch.* — In the very ancient churches to which chancels are attached, the connecting arch is

invariably semicircular, square-edged, and plain. It is usually formed of stones pretty equal in size, well hammered, and admirably fitted to each other. The greater number of primitive Irish churches, however, have no chancel, their plan being a simple oblong.

4. *Belfries.*—The *Cloig-theach*, or round tower, appears to have been the most usual belfry. The ancient structure at Glendalough, called St. Kevin's Kitchen, supports upon its western gable a small tower which appears to have answered this purpose. Bell-turrets, properly speaking, were not common before the thirteenth century.

5. *Masonry.*—Generally of very large stones, well fitted together, as in Cyclopean work. In some of the oldest examples no mortar appears to have been used, but these instances are very rare, and mortar is generally found cementing enormous stones, but never in large quantities.

6. *Roofs.*—The roofs of most of the ancient Irish churches have long disappeared, but several of stone still remain. Their pitch is exceedingly high, and they are sometimes constructed upon arches. Examples of this kind occur in St. Columb's House at Kells, in Cormac's Chapel at Cashel, in St. Kevin's Kitchen at Glendalough, and in a few other structures.

Such are the more usual and prominent characteristics of the early Irish churches. It should be observed that the doorway, with few exceptions, is almost always found to occupy a position in the centre of the west end. The windows in chancelled churches are generally five in number; one in the eastern gable, and one in each of the side walls of the nave and choir.

I shall now direct my reader's attention to the most remarkable example in the immediate vicinity of Dublin, viz., the church of Killiney.* This ruin is situated near the village of the same name, at a distance of about nine miles from the metropolis, and less than half - a - mile from Killiney station, on the Dublin, Wicklow, and Wexford Railway, and will be found particularly interesting to the student of Irish church architecture. Its extreme dimensions upon the interior are 35 feet; the nave measures but 12 feet and 8 inches; and the chancel 9 feet and 6 inches

Doorway of the Ancient Church of Killiney, Co. Dublin.

in breadth. The church originally consisted of a simple nave and choir, lighted in the usual manner, and connected by a semicircular arch; but at a period long subsequent to its original foundation, an addition, the architecture of which it will be well to compare with that of the more ancient building, has been made on the northern side. The original doorway, which, as usual, is placed in the centre of the west gable, is

* The churchyard gate is usually locked, but the key can be procured from a caretaker who resides in the neighbouring village.

remarkable for having a cross sculptured on the under part of its lintel. It measures in height 6 feet and 1 inch; in breadth at the top 2 feet; and at the bottom 2 feet 4 inches. The next feature to be noticed is the choir arch. This, which may be looked upon as a most characteristic example of its class, measures in breadth, where the arch begins to spring,

Choir Arch of the Ancient Church of Killiney, Co. Dublin.

4 feet 7 inches, and at the base 4 feet 10½ inches; its height is only 6½ feet. The chancel windows display the inclined sides, so indicative of antiquity when found in Irish ecclesiastical remains, but, with the exception of that facing the east, they are in a state of great dilapidation. The eastern window is square-headed both within and without, and exhibits the usual splay. The comparatively modern addition

on the northern side of the nave, which appears to have
been erected as a kind of aisle, is connected with the
original church by several openings broken through the
north side wall. It will be well to compare its architectural features with those of the older structure.
The pointed doorway offers a striking contrast to that
in the west gable, and its eastern window is equally
different from that in the an-
cient chancel, being larger,
and chamfered upon the exterior. The fact of a semicircular arch-head being cut out
of a single stone is of itself no
proof of high antiquity, as it
occurs in many comparatively
late structures in Ireland; and
in England I recollect to have
seen in the "Perpendicular"
church of Kirkthorpe, near
Wakefield, a door-head that
exhibited this mode of construction.

Pointed Doorway in Killiney
Church.

The church of Kilternan, situated near the little
village of Golden Ball, about six miles from Dublin,
on the Enniskerry road, presents several features of
considerable interest. The south side-wall and the
west gable are original, and of great antiquity. The
latter contains a square-headed doorway, now stopped
up with masonry; and to supply its place a pointed
entrance has been inserted in the south side-wall.

This alteration was made probably at the time of the re-erection of the eastern end, the style of which indicates a period not earlier than the close of the thirteenth century, about which time the custom of placing the doorway in the west end appears to have ceased. There are several other churches in the immediate neighbourhood of Dublin which contain features of very high antiquity, but they have been altered and remodelled at various times, and are, upon the whole, characteristic of later periods. Some of these we shall notice when describing the early pointed style, as found in Irish remains, confining our remarks for the present to such examples of the primitive ecclesiastical architecture of Ireland as are easy of access from Dublin.

Glendalough, Co. Wicklow.—The lone and singularly picturesque valley of Glendalough, in the county of Wicklow, lying at a distance of about twenty-four miles from the metropolis, presents a scene which, for stern and desolate grandeur, is in many respects unsurpassed. Huge, gloomy mountains, upon which clouds almost continually rest, encompass, and in some places overhang, the silent and almost uninhabited glen.* Two little lakes, now appearing in the deepest shadow, now reflecting the blue vault, according as the clouds above them come or go—a winding stream, and gray rocks

---

* Since the above was written Glendalough has greatly changed. A considerable number of houses have been built in and about the village ; and there is an excellent hotel. Visitors from Dublin can easily arrive at the ancient City by rail, and a short drive by car or van. See "Guide to Wicklow," published by Hodges, Figgis, & Co.

jutting here and there from out the heath—form its natural features.   A noble monastic establishment, round which a City subsequently rose, flourished, and decayed, was founded here in the early part of the sixth century by St. Kevin.   The ruins of many ecclesiastical structures yet remain, and "the long continuous shadow of the lofty and slender Round Tower moves slowly from morn till eve over wasted churches, crumbling oratories, shattered crosses, scathed yew trees, and tombs, now undistinguishable, of bishops, abbots, and anchorites."   How few of the gay tourists by whom the glen is yearly visited view these ruins with any other feeling than that of idle and ignorant curiosity ! Their ears have been poisoned with the burlesque and lying tales (inventions of the last century), which the wretched men and women, miscalled guides, of the place, have composed for the entertainment of the thoughtless.   They wander unmoved among shrines which, nearly thirteen centuries ago, were raised in honour of their God by men joyous and thankful in the feeling of certain immortality—men whose fathers in their youth had reverenced the Druid as a more than human counsellor.

That several of the existing churches formed part of the original foundation, their style of architecture sufficiently indicates.

The noble doorway of "The Lady's Church," a modern name, is, perhaps, the grandest of the kind remaining, and exhibits in a striking degree that early Greek form which is so very commonly found in the doorways and in other openings of our most ancient churches and round towers, and even, though more rudely developed, in the cathairs (cahers), and other Irish remains of the Pagan era.

Doorway of Lady's Church, Glendalough.

The remarkable building called St. Kevin's Kitchen—now, alas! sadly mutilated—is not the least interesting object in the group. Its high-pitched roof of stone remains in a perfect state. A doorway in the western gable displays an instance of the lintel surmounted by an arch. The chancel, which a few years ago remained, though of great antiquity and stone-roofed, appears to have been an addition; and a portion of the ancient east window may still be observed in the wall, just above the head of the choir arch, which was not formed in the usual manner, but *cut out* of the masonry. The little tower upon the west end appears to be the earliest example of a belfry springing from a roof or gable; but this, as well as the sacristy, is of later date than the rest of the building.

St. Kevin's " Kitchen," Glendalough.

Trinity Church, perhaps in a greater degree than any coeval structure in Leinster, retains the original character of its various parts. It possesses a magnificent specimen of the square-headed doorway; a choir arch, of its class certainly the finest in Ireland; chancel windows, with heads semicircular or triangular; in fact almost every characteristic of the more ancient style of church architecture in Ireland, and each perfect in its way. There was formerly a round tower belfry attached to the western end.

In that singularly interesting ruin, styled the Monastery, are columns which, upon their capitals, exhibit ornamental sculpture of a style peculiar to monuments of the ninth and tenth centuries. These in England would usually be pronounced Norman, more particularly as the arch which they were designed to sustain displays a variety of the zig-zag or chevron moulding, as may be seen from several of its stones which yet remain. This arch has, in a great measure, been recently restored.

The Refeart, or Royal Cemetery Church, though less imposing in its general appearance than several of the equally ancient remains in the more eastern part of the glen, is, on account of its association with the life of the founder, not surpassed in interest by any of the others.

In the cemetery of this (Refeart) church was preserved, about half a century since, an ancient inscribed tombstone, popularly called King O'Toole's Monument; but it has long disappeared, "the guides" having sold it in small pieces to tourists scarcely less ignorant than themselves.

The large structure, standing within the enclosure of the cemetery, a little eastward from the round tower, is popularly styled "the Cathedral," and appears, from its name, dimensions, and position, to have been anciently the *Domnach mor*, or *Daimhliag-mor*, or chief church of the place. Notwithstanding its present state of dilapidation, there are in Ireland few structures of the same antiquity and extent that retain so many

original features. The tower adjoining is one of the
largest and most perfectly-preserved now remaining.
Its semicircular doorway-head, carved out of a single
stone, may be looked upon as a good example of that
peculiar mode of construction.

A *caiseal*, or wall, appears usually to have enclosed
the greater number of the ancient Irish monastic establishments. That such a work anciently existed at
Glendalough is certain, though scarcely a vestige of it
at present remains above ground. One of the gateways, however, until very lately, stood in a nearly
perfect state. It is described and engraved by Dr.
Petrie on the "Round Towers," page 447, and his
prophecy, that for want of care this monument, unique
in its kind, would soon cease to exist, became half-
fulfilled shortly after upon the fall of the principal
arch. The stones, however, have been re-set, and the
work possesses much of its pristine appearance.

I have but slightly glanced at the greater and more
generally interesting ruins of this celebrated glen. It
also contains numerous relics, such as crosses, monumental stones, &c., which by a visitor should not be
overlooked; but as I shall have occasion to refer my
readers to other and much finer remains of each class
of antiquities which they represent, it would be at least
unnecessary to describe them here. I may, however,
mention the singular chamber called " St. Kevin's Bed."
That it is altogether a work of art cannot be satisfactorily demonstrated. Though, to a certain degree,
its artificial character is distinctly marked, it is quite

possible that a natural cavity, the sides of which have been roughly hewn and squared, may have existed previously. The Bed, which is situated in an almost overhanging rock, at a considerable distance above the lake, is said to have been the residence of St. Kevin at some period, when pursuing that course of study and contemplation for which his name, even to this day, is revered; and the celebrated St. Laurence O'Toole is said to have spent much of his time in prayer and heavenly contemplation in this cavern.

St. Columb's House, Kells.—One of the earliest examples of cylindrical vaulting remaining in Ireland occurs in the structure called St. Columb's House, at Kells, county of Meath. The arch, which is completely devoid of ornament, springs from the side walls, and separates the body of the building from a small croft to which access was anciently gained by a quadrangular opening, about 19 inches in breadth, adjoining the west gable. Two walls, crossing and resting upon this arch, and pierced each with a small semicircular-headed doorway, together with the gables, support a roof of stone. The lower apartment was lighted by two windows, one in the centre of the east end, the other in the south side-wall. Both windows are small, and splay inwardly. That to the east is formed with a semicircular arch, while the other presents a triangular head. The ancient doorway, which was elevated, in the west end, has been almost obliterated. St. Columb's House is supposed to have combined the purpose of an oratory with that of a habitation, and in this respect to class with St. Kevin's House, or Kitchen, at Glendalough, St. Flannan's House at Killaloe, and one or two other structures. Whether we regard

St. Columb's House at Kells, Co. Meath.

it as a habitation, or as a church, to which purpose this, in common with similar buildings, was certainly through many ages applied, it is a ruin of no common interest; and I strongly recommend such of my readers as may have a day or two to spare to visit Kells. The round tower adjoining, and the various crosses in the cemetery and in the market-place, afford severally an admirable study. The latter are only inferior in size to the beautiful remains at Monasterboice, of which notice will be found in a subsequent chapter.

Window in St. Columb's House.

(From the interior.)

CHAPTER III.

EARLY DECORATED CHURCHES.

CHURCH OF KILLESHIN—EXAMPLES AT RAHAN—CORMACK'S CHAPEL
AT CASHEL.

HURCHES like those to which reference
has just been made are such, as we
have every reason to believe, were
generally constructed during the earlier
ages of Christianity in this kingdom.
How long the style continued is a matter of
very great uncertainty. The horizontal lintel appears
gradually to have given place to the semicircular arch-
head. The high-pitched roof becomes flattened, the
walls lose much of their Cyclopean character, and in
several examples a considerable quantity of cement
appears to have been used. The windows exhibit a
slight recess, or a chamfer, upon the exterior, and are
of greater size; a small bead-moulding is occasionally
found extending round an arch upon the interior. The
walls are generally higher, and of somewhat inferior
masonry. As the style advanced the sides of the doorways became cut into a series of recesses, the angles of
which were slightly rounded off. The addition of a

slight moulding, at first a mere incision, upon the piers, would seem to have suggested pillars. Chevron and other decorations, which in England are supposed to indicate the Norman period, are commonly found, but they are generally simple lines cut upon the face and soffit of the arch. Pediments now appear, and the various mouldings and other details of doorways and other openings become rich and striking, and, in some respects, bear considerable analogy to true Norman work. The capitals frequently represent human heads, the hair of which is interlaced with snake-like animals. A similar style of decoration is displayed upon the features of several of the round towers, as at Timahoe. The church of Killeshin, in the Queen's County, lying at a distance of about two miles from Carlow, appears to have been one of the most beautiful structures of this class ever erected in Ireland. Its doorway, until very lately, retained in a remarkable degree the original sharpness of its sculpture. I was informed that many years ago a resident in the neighbourhood used to take pleasure in destroying, as far as lay in his power, the interesting capitals here represented, and that to his labours, and not to the effects of time, we may attribute the almost total obliteration of an Irish inscription which formerly extended round the abacus, and of which but few letters at present remain.

It appears that within the last half century there has been a greater destruction of Irish antiquities through sheer wantonness than the storms, and frost, and light-

ning of ages could have accomplished. Such acts of
Vandalism have not always been perpetrated by the
unlettered peasant. Indeed, the devotional feeling

Capitals at Killeshin.

of the labouring classes of the greater part of Ireland leads them to regard antiquities, especially

Capitals at Killeshin.

those of an ecclesiastical origin, with a feeling of
veneration. These outrages have most frequently
been committed by "conservers," by contractors for
the erection of new buildings for the sake of the
stones, or, for the same reason, by men of station

and education, who should have recollected that age
and neglect cannot deprive structures, once consecrated to God and applied to the service of religion, of
any portion of their sacred character. The church of
Killeshin is, perhaps, late in the style. The arches
(there are four concentric), which form the doorway,
display a great variety of ornamental detail, consisting
of chevron work, animals, &c., &c. A pediment sur-

mounts the external arch; and a window in the south side-wall is canopied by a broad band, ascending and
converging in straight lines. A window of similar construction appears
in the Round Tower of Timahoe.
Perhaps one of the most remarkable
specimens of this style of church remaining, occurs at Rahan, near Tulla-
more, in the King's County. It is

Window at Killeshin.

minutely described and illustrated by
Dr. Petrie in pp. 240, 241 of the work to which I
have so frequently alluded. It appears from historical
evidence to belong to the eighth century. A triple
choir arch, and a circular window, highly ornamented, are the chief remaining details of the original building. The piers of the former are rounded
off into semi-columns, with capitals of very singular
character, totally distinct from Norman work. The
bases are globular in form, and are sculptured in each
compartment out of a single stone. The capitals or
imposts are ornamented upon their angles with human

heads, the hair of which is carried back and represented by shallow lines cut upon the face of the stone in a very fanciful manner.

The window, which is 7 feet 6 inches in diameter, is composed of stones unequal in size, and displaying chevron ornaments in very low relief.

It is a fact well worthy of observation that the details which I have mentioned as characteristic of this style are never found associated with others known to belong exclusively to the Norman period.

The Rock of Cashel.—The Great Southern and Western Railway brings Cashel within a few

The Rock of Cashel.

hours' journey of the metropolis; and as the ruins upon the celebrated Rock are unparalleled, at least in Ireland, for picturesque beauty and antiquarian interest, there are few by whom a visit to the place would not be remembered with pleasure.

Cormac's chapel, which, with the exception of the round tower, is the most ancient structure of the group, was built by Cormac Mac Carthy, King of Munster, in the beginning of the twelfth century. It is roofed with stone, and in its capitals, arches, and other features and details, the Hiberno-Romanesque style is distinctly marked.

The plan is a nave and chancel, with a square tower on either side, at their junction. The southern tower is ornamented externally with six projecting bands, three of which are continued along the side walls of the structure, and it is finished at the top by a plain parapet, the masonry of which is different from that of the other portions, and evidently of a later period. The northern tower remains in its original state, and is covered with a pyramidical cap of stone.

An almost endless variety of Hiberno-Romanesque decorations appear upon the arches, and other features of the building, both within and without. Both nave and chancel are roofed with a semicircular arch, resting upon square ribs, which spring from a series of massive semi-columns, set at equal distances against the walls. The bases of these semi-columns are on a level with the capitals of the choir-arch, the abacus of which is continued as a string course round the interior of the building.

The walls of both nave and chancel beneath the string course are ornamented with a row of semicircular arches, slightly recessed, and enriched with chevron, billet, and other ornaments and mouldings.

Those of the nave spring from square imposts resting upon piers, while those in the chancel have pillars and well-formed capitals. There are small crofts to which access is gained by a spiral stair in the southern tower, between the arches over both nave and chancel and the external roof. These little apartments were probably used as dormitories by the ecclesiastics. A somewhat similar croft in the church of St. Dolough's, near Dublin, is furnished with a fire-place, a fact which clearly demonstrates that they were applied to the purpose of a habitation.

The doorways of Cormac's chapel are three in number—one in the centre of the west end, and one in each of the side walls of the nave, within a few feet of the west gable. The northern and southern doorways are original, and are headed with a tympanum or lintel between the aperture and the semicircular arches above. They are both exceedingly rich in sculpture, but the northern doorway appears to have been the chief entrance, as it is considerably larger and more highly decorated than the other. It is surmounted with a canopy; and the tympanum is sculptured with a very singular device, representing a combat between a centaur, armed with bow and arrow, and a huge animal, probably intended for a lion. The head of the centaur is covered by a conical helmet with a nasal, and he is shooting a barbed arrow into the breast of the lion. A small animal beneath the feet of the latter appears to have been slain in the encounter.

The western doorway is not canopied, and its

tympanum is sculptured with a single animal, not unlike the lion upon the other.

As recorded in our annals Cormac's chapel was consecrated in A.D. 1134, with great ceremony. There can, therefore, be no question as to the age of this beautiful structure, which is said, on competent authority, to be equal to anything in England or Normandy of the same class and period.

It is interesting to remark that the first Anglo-Norman invasion of Ireland occurred in A.D. 1171–72, thirty-seven years later than the act of consecration referred to.

At Cashel, the perfect round tower; Cormac's chapel; the magnificent cathedral founded by Donogh O'Brien, King of Thomond, *circa* 1152; the ancient castle of the archbishops; Hoar Abbey, situated upon the plain immediately beside the Rock—and the numerous crosses and other remains—afford most valuable studies for the architectural antiquary or the artist.

CHAPTER IV.

CROSSES.

VARIETIES OF THE EARLY CROSSES—EXAMPLE AT MONASTERBOICE—
THEIR SCULPTURE AND DECORATIONS — MONUMENTAL STONES —
ANCIENT CHRISTIAN GRAVES — EXAMPLES AT ST. JOHN'S POINT,
ARRANGED IN CIRCLES.

ET us now glance at the graves of Erin's
early saints, which are usually marked by
stones differing in nowise from the pagan
pillar stone, except that in some instances
they are sculptured with a cross, plain, or
within a circle. This style of memorial appears to
have been succeeded by a rudely-formed cross, the
arms of which are little more than indicated, and which
is usually fixed in a socket, cut in a large, flat stone.
Such crosses rarely exhibit any kind of ornament, but
occasionally, even in very rude examples, the upper
part of the shaft is hewn into the form of a circle, from
which the arms and top extend; and those portions
of the stone by which the circle is indicated, are
frequently perforated, or slightly recessed. A fine
plain cross of this style may be seen on the road
adjoining the grave-yard of Tullagh, Co. Dublin;
and there is an early-decorated example near the

church of Finglas, in the same county. Crosses highly
sculptured appear to have been very generally erected
between the ninth and twelfth centuries ; but there are
few examples of a later date remaining, if we except a
small number bearing inscriptions in Latin or English,
which generally belong to the close of the sixteenth, or
to the seventeenth century, and which can hardly be
looked upon as either Irish or ancient.

From the rude pillar stone, marked with the symbol
of our faith, enclosed within a circle, the emblem of
eternity, the finely-proportioned and elaborately-sculp-
tured crosses of a later period are derived. In the
latter the circle, instead of being simply cut upon the
face of the stone, is represented by a ring binding, as
it were, the shaft, arms, and upper portion of the cross
together.

Crosses at Monasterboice.—The beautiful remains of this class at Monasterboice, near Drogheda—
though the finest now remaining in Ireland—are nearly
equalled by many others scattered over the whole island.
Indeed in our crosses alone we have evidence sufficient
to satisfy the most sceptical of the skill which the Irish
had attained, in more of the arts than one, during the
earlier ages of the Church. They may be regarded,
not only as memorials of the piety and munificence of
a people—whom ignorance and prejudice have too often
sneered at as barbarous—but also as the finest works of
sculptured art, of their period, now existing.

Two crosses at Monasterboice remain in their ancient
position, and are well preserved, though one of them,

in particular, bears distinct evidence of a systematic
attempt having been made to destroy it. A third has
been broken to pieces—the people say by Cromwell—
but its head and part of the shaft remaining uninjured,
the fragment has been re-set in its ancient socket.*

The Great Cross, Monasterboice.

The largest of the two more perfect crosses measures
27 feet in height, and is composed of three stones.
Some feet of the base is buried in the soil. The shaft
at its junction with the base is 2 feet in breadth, and

* See p. 182, where its central boss is figured.

1 foot 3 inches in thickness. It is divided upon the
western side by fillets into seven compartments, each
of which contains two or more figures executed with
bold effect, but much worn by the rain and wind of
nearly nine centuries. The sculpture of the first compartment, beginning at the base, has been destroyed by
those who attempted to throw down the monument.
The second contains four figures, of which one, apparently the most important, is presenting a book to
another, who receives it with both hands, while a
large bird seems resting upon his head. The other
figures in this compartment represent females, one of
whom holds a child in her arms.

Compartments 3, 4, 5, and 6 contain three figures
each, evidently the Apostles, and each figure is represented as holding a book. The seventh division, which
runs into the circle forming the head of the cross, is
occupied by two figures; and immediately above them
is a representation of our Saviour crucified, while a
soldier upon each side is piercing his body with a
spear. To the right and to the left of the figure of
our Saviour other sculptures appear. The figures upon
the right arm of the cross are represented apparently
in the act of adoration. The action of those upon the
left is obscure, and in consequence of the greater expo-
sure of the upper portion of the stone to the weather,
the sculpture which it bears is much worn, and almost
effaced.

The sides of the shaft are ornamented with figures
and scroll-work, placed alternately in compartments

one above the other. Of the circle by which the arms
and stem are connected, the ex-
ternal edges are enriched; and
as an example I have engraved
the compartment beneath the left
arm. The eastern side is also
divided into compartments occupied by sculptures, which may
refer to Scripture history.

The smaller cross is most emi-
nently beautiful. The figures
and ornaments with which its
various sides are enriched appear
to have been executed with an
unusual degree of care, and even

Ornament beneath Arm of the
Great Cross, Monasterboice.

of artistic skill. It has suffered but little from the
effects of time. The sacrilegious hands which attempted
the ruin of the others appear to have spared this, and it
stands almost as perfect as when, nearly nine centuries
ago, the artist we may suppose pronounced his work
finished ; and chiefs and abbots, bards, shanachies, warriors, ecclesiastics, and perhaps many a rival sculptor,
crowded round this very spot—full of wonder and
admiration for what they must have considered a
truly glorious and perhaps unequalled work.

An inscription in Irish, upon the lower part of the
shaft, desires " a prayer for Muiredach, by whom was
made this cross"; but as Dr. Petrie, by whom the
inscription has been published, remarks there were two
of the name mentioned in the Irish Annals as having

been connected with Monasterboice—one an abbot, who died in the year 844, and the other in the year 924—"so that it must be a matter of some uncertainty to which of these the erection of the cross should be ascribed." There is reason, however, to assign it to the latter, "as he was a man of greater distinction, and

Cross of Muiredach, sometimes called the Smaller Cross, Monasterboice.

probably wealth, than the former, and therefore more likely to have been the erector of the crosses." Its total height is exactly 15 ft., and it is 6 ft. in breadth at the arms. The shaft, which at the base measures in breadth 2½ ft. and in thickness 1 ft. 9 in., diminishes slightly in its ascent, and is divided upon its various

sides by twisted bands into compartments, each of
which contains either sculptured figures or tracery of
very intricate design, or animals, probably symbolical.

The figures and other carvings retain almost unim-
paired their original sharpness and beauty of execution.

The former are of great
interest, as affording an
excellent idea of the dress,
both ecclesiastical and military, of the Irish during
the ninth and tenth cen-
turies. As an example, I
give the two lower com-
partments upon the west
side. Within the circular
head of the cross, upon its
eastern face, our Saviour
is represented sitting in
judgment. A choir of
angels occupy the arm to
the right of the figure.
Several are represented
with musical instruments,
among which the ancient
Irish harp may be seen :

Portion of the Sculpture on the Cross
of Muiredach.

it is small and triangular, and rests upon the knees
of the performer, who is represented in a sitting
posture. The space to the left of our Saviour is
crowded with figures, several of which are in an attitude of despair. They are the damned; and an armed

fiend is driving them from before the throne. The compartment immediately beneath bears a figure weighing in a pair of huge scales a smaller figure, the balance seeming to preponderate in his favour. One who appears to have been weighed, and found wanting, is lying beneath the scales in an attitude of terror. The next compartment beneath represents, apparently, the adoration of the Wise Men. The star above the head of the infant Christ is distinctly marked. The third compartment contains several figures, the action of which I do not understand. The signification of the sculpture of the next following compartment is also very obscure : a figure seated upon a throne or chair is blowing a horn, and soldiers with conical helmets, armed with short broad-bladed swords, and with small circular shields, appear crowding in. The fifth and lowest division illustrates the Temptation and the Expulsion. The figures upon the western face of the

Boss of Cross, Monasterboice.

shaft, of which I have engraved two compartments, probably relate to the early history of Monasterboice. The head of the cross upon this side is sculptured with a Crucifixion, very similar to that upon the head of the larger cross, but the execution is better. Its northern arm underneath bears the representation of a hand extended, and holding what Wright, in his "Louth-iana," calls a cake, probably the Host.   Of the broken cross I have engraved a boss, placed within its circle. It is otherwise plain.

An early monumental stone remains in the cemetery, a few yards to the north of the less ancient church. The inscription is in the Irish language and character, and reads in English, " A prayer for Ruarchan."   A simple flagstone, inscribed with a name, and sculptured with the sacred symbol of Christianity—such as it was the custom among the early Irish Christians to place over the grave of an emi-nent man—forms a striking contrast to the tablets which too often disfigure the walls of our cathedral and parish churches.   Many remains of

Inscribed Tombstone, Inis Cealtra.

this class lie scattered among the ancient and often-neglected graveyards of Ireland ; but they are every day becoming more rare, as the country stone-cutters, by whom they are regarded with but slight veneration, frequently form out of their materials modern tombstones, defacing the ancient inscription. I have engraved a characteristic example from Inis Cealtra, an island in Lough Derg, an expansion of the Shannon.

In several cemeteries found in connexion with the
earlier monastic establishments of Ireland, graves
formed after the pagan fashion—of flat stones placed
edgeways in an oblong figure, and covered with large
flags—frequently occur.   But that in several instances
the stones at either end of the enclosure have been
sculptured with a cross, they might be supposed to
indicate the site of a pagan cemetery, which the early
Christians, for obvious reasons, had hallowed by the
erection of a *cill*.   The direction of the grave is
generally east and west; but in the cemetery adjoining the very early church at Saint John's Point, in the
county of Down, and elsewhere, the cists are arranged
in the form of a circle, to the centre of which the feet
of the dead converge.

A similar mode of interment, which occurs at Town-
y-Chapel, near Holyhead, in Wales, is referred to in
the "Archæological Journal," vol. iii.; and it is worthy
of remark, that the place where the graves are found
appears to have been the scene of a battle, fought about
A. D. 450, in which many Irishmen were slain.

CHAPTER V.

ROUND TOWERS.

OPINIONS FORMERLY CURRENT WITH REGARD TO THE ORIGIN AND
USES OF THE ROUND TOWERS—THEIR CHARACTERISTICS—DOORWAYS,
WINDOWS, AND APERTURES—EXAMPLES AT CLONDALKIN, MONASTER-
BOICE, KILDARE, AND DONOUGHMORE.

OUND TOWERS of about 18 feet in external
diameter, and varying in height between
60 and 115 feet, are frequently found in
connexion with the earlier monastic establishments of Ireland. The question of their
origin and uses has long occupied much antiquarian
attention. In the seventeenth and eighteenth centuries
they had been regarded by our antiquaries as the work
of the Danes ; but towards the close of the last century
General Vallancey propounded various theories, which
assumed them to be of Phœnician or Indo-Scythic
origin, and to have contained the sacred fire from
whence all the fires in the kingdom were annually
rekindled. But Vallancey was very unsteady in his
opinions, and his successors multiplied their theories
till they became almost as numerous as the towers
themselves ; and each succeeding writer, instead of
elucidating, appeared to involve the subject in deeper

mystery than ever—a mystery that was proverbial, till dispelled completely and for ever by Dr. Petrie in his beautiful and splendid work, which has justly been judged as " the most learned, the most exact, and the

Antrim Round Tower.

most important ever published upon the antiquities of the ancient Irish nation."

The following are Dr. Petrie's conclusions :—

1. That the towers are of Christian and ecclesiastical origin, and were erected at various periods between the fifth and thirteenth centuries.

2. That they were designed to answer, at least, a twofold use, namely, to serve as belfries, and as keeps, or places of strength, in which the sacred utensils, books, relics, and other valuables, were deposited, and into which the ecclesiastics to whom they belonged could retire for security in cases of sudden attack.

3. That they were probably also used, when occasion required, as beacons and watch-towers.

That these conclusions were arrived at after a long and patient investigation, not only of the architectural peculiarities of the numerous round towers, but also of the ecclesiastical structures usually found in connexion with them, is sufficiently shown by many references to and illustrations of examples scattered over the whole island. But Dr. Petrie also, with the assistance of the best Celtic scholars in Ireland, sought in our annals and in our ancient MSS. (fortunately not a few) for references to such buildings as it was the custom of the Irish to erect; and from this hitherto-neglected source of information much of the light which he has thrown upon the subject of ancient Irish ecclesiology has been derived. But to our subject. There is but little variety to be observed in the construction or details of the round towers. The following is a summary of their usual features :—

Doorways. — In form similar to those we have described as characteristic of the early churches, but they are generally more highly ornamented, and appear to have been furnished with double doors. They are placed almost invariably at a considerable elevation above the ground. A flat projecting band, with a small bead-moulding at the angles, is the most usual decoration; but in some instances a human head,

Cross over the Doorway of Antrim Tower.

sculptured in bold relief, is found upon each side of the arch. A stone immediately above the doorway of

Sculpture over Doorway of Donoughmore Tower, Co. Meath.

Antrim tower exhibits a cross sculptured in *alto-relievo;* and at Donoughmore, in Co. Meath, a figure of the Crucifixion, in bold relief, occupies a similar position.

This style of decoration may have been much more common than is generally supposed, as of the number of towers remaining in Ireland the doorways of at least one-third have been destroyed. Concentric arches, with chevron and other mouldings, occur at Timahoe and at Kildare.

Clondalkin Round Tower.

Windows and Apertures. — Generally similar in form to those in contemporaneous churches, with this difference, that they never splay, and that the arch-head in numerous examples is of a different form upon the interior from the exterior. The tower was usually divided into stories, the floors of which were supported by projections of the masonry or by brackets. Each

story, except the highest, was generally lighted by
one small window: the highest has generally four of
large size. A conical roof of stone completed the
building.

In the village of Clondalkin, at a distance of about
four miles from Dublin, and adjoining a station of the
Great Southern and Western Railway, stands one of the
most preserved of the Round Towers. Its height to the

top of the cone is 90 feet.
The doorway, which is ap-
proached by a flight of stone
steps, comparatively mo-
dern, is square-headed, and
perfectly plain, as are also
the windows and top aper-
tures. Some years ago a
gentleman of the neigh-
bourhood caused this tower
to be repaired, upon which
occasion floors were added,
and placed in their ancient
position. Access may be had

Doorway of Clondalkin Tower.

from story to story by the aid of fixed ladders, so that
a visitor has here an opportunity for observation not
frequently to be met with. It should be remarked that
the projection at the base is not found in any other
instance, and that it may possibly be an after-work.
The tower of Clondalkin, though nearly perfect, cannot
be considered a very fine example of its class. It is
somewhat low, and its roof, which does not appear to

be original, is wanting in that degree of lightness and elegance observable in many.

The other towers in the immediate neighbourhood of Dublin are at Swords, Lusk, and Rathmichael. The last is a mere stump, and as the others do not present

General View of Monasterboice.

any point of attraction not equally to be found at Clondalkin, I shall refer my readers to the noble example at Monasterboice, within four miles and a-half of Drogheda. The churches, the tower, and the magnificent crosses of this ancient seat of piety and learning, form a group of ecclesiastical antiquities in many respects unsurpassed in Ireland. A description of the crosses will be found in a previous chapter.

The tower, the erection of which there is every reason to refer to a very early period, is one of peculiar and striking interest, exhibiting, as it does, a decorated doorway, the head of which is cut out of two stones laid horizontally one above the other. A band extends round the head and down the sides of the doorway, but terminates on a level with the sill, or rather turns off at a right angle, passing horizontally for a distance of eight inches, from which point it ascends, and running upwards round the doorway head, gives the appearance of a double band. A space between the bands, upon each side of the upper part of the doorway, and one upon the semicircular arched head, left uncut, appear suggestive of the cross. The window immediately over the doorway may be looked upon as a characteristic example of the opening found in a similar position in most of the towers, and which is supposed to have answered the purpose of a second doorway, or to have been designed for the purpose of affording persons within the tower some means of defending the entrance beneath. In this example, however, it is unusually small. The other windows are square-headed, as were also the large apertures of the uppermost story.* The masonry is good, and characteristic of a very early period; the stones large, well fitted together, and passing through a considerable thickness of the wall, as may be observed in the upper portion of the structure, where a considerable rent has been made.†

* See Wright's *Louthiana*, Plate 14, Book iii.
† Since the above was penned the tower has been well repaired.

A church of very primitive construction, and probably several centuries older than the tower, stands in the cemetery, at a little distance to the north-east of the other remains. Its only doorway is placed, as usual, in the centre of the west gable. It is square-headed, and possesses every indication of a high antiquity, but the accumulation of the churchyard soil has buried the lower portion at least to a depth of several feet. The church presented anciently the nave and chancel; the latter has been destroyed, but a plain semicircular chancel arch remains. The church immediately adjoining the round tower is obviously an erection of the early part of the thirteenth century.*

The student of antiquities, by taking an early train from Dublin, may examine the ruins of Kildare, Carlow, and Killeshin, and return the same day.†

The round tower of Kildare is in several respects one of the most remarkable in Ireland. Its doorway, of which an illustration is annexed, is unusually rich, consisting of three concentric arches, upon two of which a variety of mouldings appear. The external arch is quite plain, and evidently not as ancient as the others. An ornamental canopy, a portion of which still remains, anciently surmounted the doorway. This tower, it should be observed, is unusually large, and bears evidence of having been repaired at various periods.

* For a notice of the crosses of this most interesting locality see part ii., chap. iv., p. 177.

† See p. 169.

Like the round tower of Cloyne, in the county of
Cork, and like those of Kilkenny, and Kilmallock, it
is finished with a plain battlemented parapet, comparatively modern, and added, probably, at some
period when the original roof of stone had lately been
destroyed by lightning or by other means. In a former

Doorway of Kildare Tower.

chapter I noticed the singularly interesting group of
early ecclesiastical structures remaining in the valley
of Glendalough, in the county of Wicklow.   The
round tower, a work apparently coeval with the
" Cathedral," may be looked upon as one of the most
characteristic now to be found in Leinster. The towers
of Clondalkin, Swords, and Lusk may.be easily visited

by car or rail from Dublin.   There is a station close to
Lusk, on the Great Northern Railway.   The best plan
would be to proceed to Malahide, where cars are always
to be had on hire.   The towers of Lusk and Swords
might be reached after a comparatively short drive.

Such readers as may be induced to visit the antiquities of Dowth and Newgrange, are recommended
to extend their drive as far as Donoughmore, near
Navan, where they will find a tower interesting in
many points, but particularly so as the stone which
forms the crown of its doorway arch, and the one
directly above it, are sculptured with a figure of the
Crucifixion, as represented in p. 188.   They might
take in on their direct way the great tumulus of
Knowth (similar to those of Newgrange and Dowth),
as well as the beautiful Abbey of Slane, St. Erc's
Hermitage in Slane Demesne, and the interesting
Castle of Dunmoe, formerly a stronghold of the
Darcys.   If they pushed on to Navan, just one mile
beyond Donoughmore, they could inspect a grand
old castle of the Dowdalls, and return to Dublin by
train.

PART III.

𝔄𝔫𝔤𝔩𝔬-𝔍𝔯𝔦𝔰𝔥 𝔊𝔢𝔪𝔞𝔦𝔫𝔰.

CHAPTER I.

ABBEYS, ETC.

JERPOINT ABBEY, CO. KILKENNY—CATHEDRALS OF ST. PATRICK AND
CHRIST CHURCH, DUBLIN—ABBEYS OF NEWTOWN AND BECTIVE, NEAR
TRIM, CO. MEATH—CHURCHES OF CANNISTOWN, NEAR NAVAN—
ST. DOULOUGH'S, NEAR DUBLIN—HOWTH "ABBEY"—ST. FENTON'S,
OR ST. FINTAN'S CHURCH, HOWTH.

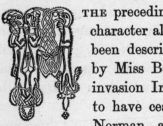 THE preceding chapters monuments of a
character almost peculiar to Ireland have
been described. It has been remarked
by Miss Beaufort that at the English
invasion Irish architecture may be said
to have ceased, the English or Anglo-
Norman adventurers having brought
with them their own fashion of building, which was
afterwards copied by the Irish. Certain it is that the
close of the twelfth and beginning of the thirteenth
centuries witnessed a great change in the style of
architecture as applied to ecclesiastical edifices in
Ireland; but that this change was a consequence of
the invasion, or that the pointed style was borrowed

from, or introduced into Ireland, by the English, has not been ascertained.

We have, in common with other nations, evidence of the gradual adoption of the pointed arch in our ecclesiastical structures ; and it should be observed that, for several centuries previous to the Invasion, Irish architecture had been gradually undergoing a change, and had, in some measure become, what in England is called, " Norman," or Romanesque—a style from which, or rather through which, the Pointed arose ultimately from the pure Temple architecture of Greece and Rome. Towards the close of the twelfth century the Irish kings and chiefs, and the Anglo-Norman earls and barons settled in Ireland, appear to have vied with each other in the erection of abbeys, the ruins of which, to this day, attest the zeal and power of their founders. Most of the monastic structures of this period, in their larger arches, exhibit beautiful examples of the earliest pointed style, while the doorways and smaller openings remain semi-circular, and frequently exhibit pure Norman details. Almost the last traces of peculiarly Celtic architectural art appear to have died out in Ireland about the close of the twelfth century. Chevroned pointed arches occur in the nave of Dunbrody Abbey, which was erected by Hervey De Mountmorris, and belongs to this period. The choir is generally vaulted, and lighted by three windows, exceedingly tall and narrow, and separated by massive piers, the chamfers upon the external angles of which amount to splays.

Jerpoint Abbey, in the county of Kilkenny, founded by Donogh (MacGillapatrick), King of Ossory, is, perhaps, the grandest structure of this period remaining in Ireland.

The plan of the church was cruciform, with aisles on the north side of both nave and choir. The greater portion of the southern wall has been destroyed. The western window consists of three days or lights, with semicircular heads, surmounted by a continuous weather-moulding. A fine range of clear story windows of the same character appears in the northern wall of the nave. The tower, though of very considerable antiquity, is evidently of later date than the transition period, and was probably added contemporaneously with the decorated window in the western end of the choir. The only entrance to the body of the church from the exterior appears to have been a small doorway in the south wall of the nave, and this is defended by a bartizan, or machicolation, similar to those found upon castles of the twelfth century. The transition style soon gave place to the early pointed, and our grandest existing cathedrals and abbeys almost exclusively belong to the latter. As early examples we may mention portions of Christ Church, and St. Patrick's, Dublin ; Gray Abbey, Co. Down; the Cathedral of Cashel; the Abbey of Newtown, near Trim ; and Kilmallock Abbey, Co. Limerick. Perhaps the finest window of this style in Ireland is that of the Abbey of Kilmallock. It consists of five slender lancets, separated by shafts, upon which are two sets of the bands so characteristic of this period. A large and beautifully proportioned arch embraces all the lights, which, both internally and externally, are enriched with a bead moulding.

The Cathedrals of St. Patrick and Christ Church, Dublin, have been frequently described. The former was erected, probably upon the site of an older church, by John Comyn, Archbishop of Dublin, who, according to Ware, died in 1212. Its prevailing style is early or first pointed, and it is remarkable as the only structure in Ireland having original flying buttresses. A lofty and well-proportioned tower, erected in 1370, rises from the north-west angle of the building, and supports a spire of granite, an addition of the last century, as its character sufficiently testifies.

Though in point of size and architectural grandeur, St. Patrick's cannot be compared with many structures of the same class elsewhere, it is, nevertheless, a very chaste and beautiful church. Through the princely munificence of the late Sir B. L. Guinness the building has somewhat recently been thoroughly restored.

Christ Church Cathedral was originally founded in the early part of the eleventh century, by Sitric, son of Amlave, King of the Danes of Dublin, in conjunction with Donatus, the first Danish bishop, but no portion of the present structure is of higher antiquity than the close of the twelfth century. The arches of the nave are remarkably beautiful, springing from piers formed of clustered columns, and displaying in their capitals foliage of most exquisitely graceful design. The oldest

portions of the church are the transepts, some of the
arches of which display chevron mouldings, and the
doorway, which forms the principal entrance, is completely Norman. It was removed some years ago
from the north transept, and placed in its present
position, where it forms a conspicuous feature. Christ
Church, like St. Patrick's, has of late years been
thoroughly restored. The necessary funds, amounting
to over £160,000, were supplied by H. Roe, the
eminent Dublin distiller.

To every student of the mediæval architecture of
Ireland I strongly recommend a visit to the ancient
town of Trim, not only because its neighbourhood
contains many remains of high interest, and may be
visited by rail with little expenditure of time, but also
as it forms a centre from which several excursions might
be made, Kells, Tara, and Bective lying not far off.
For the present I shall confine my remarks to some
of the antiquities of Newtown, a village situated upon
the Boyne, a little lower down than Trim. The abbey,
founded by Simon Rochfort, or de Rupeforti, for
Augustine Canons, about A. D. 1206, and dedicated to
St. Peter and St. Paul, though now in a woful state of
dilapidation, was anciently one of the grandest in this
part of the country, as may be judged from the
exquisite beauty of some of the details, such as capitals,
vaulting, shafts, &c., &c., which have not been disturbed, and from the numerous fragments of its once
noble windows and arches with which the surrounding
cemetery is strewn. Broad strips of masonry, placed

at a considerable distance apart, project from the walls
of the church upon the exterior, a feature never found
but in early work, and which is generally characteristic
of the Norman period.   But it is within the walls that
we must seek for evidence of the former beauty of the
building.   Several chastely decorated corbel shafts
remain, and support portions of the ribs by which the
vaulted roof was sustained.   The windows are of the

Newtown Abbey, near Trim, Co. Meath.

lancet form with piers between, and the mouldings
which run round them are ornamented with beautifully
designed bands.   Sedilia, in the Norman style of
architecture, may be seen in the wall to the right of
the space anciently occupied by the altar.   The ruins
on the opposite side of the river and the ancient bridge
at this place are well worthy of notice, but, as they
do not possess any striking peculiarity, we shall refer
our readers to the Abbey of Bective, in the immediate
neighbourhood of Trim, a Cistercian house, founded by

Murchard O'Melaghlin, Prince of Meath, in A.D. 1146, 1148, or 1151. These ruins combine a union of ecclesiastical with military and domestic architecture in a remarkable degree. Their chief feature is a strong battlemented tower, the lower apartment of which is vaulted, placed at the southward corner of the quadrangular space occupied by the various buildings, and

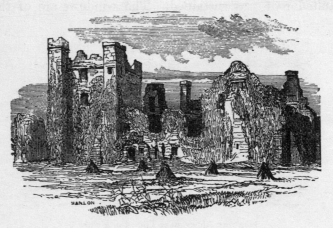

Abbey of Bective, near Trim, Co. Meath.

in the centre of which the cloisters remain in excellent preservation. The cloister arches are late in the first pointed style and are cinque-foiled. The featherings are mostly plain, but several are ornamented with flowers, or leaves, and upon one a hawk-like bird is sculptured. A fillet is worked upon each of the clustered shafts by which the openings are divided, and also upon their capitals. The bases, which are circular, rest upon square plinths, the angles of which are ornamented with a leaf, as it were, growing out of the base moulding. Of the church there are scarcely any remains. As the northern wall of the cloister is pierced with several windows which now have the appearance of splaying externally, it is extremely probable that it also served as the south wall of the church, no other portion of which can at present be identified. Those buildings which were devoted to domestic purposes are, for the most part, situated upon the east side of the quadrangle. Their architectural details are of a character later than those of the tower and of the other portions, but additions and alterations have evidently been made. Several of the apartments have large fire-places covered with flat arches, the stones of which are dove-tailed into one another. The flues are carried up through the thickness of the wall, and are continued through square tapering chimney-shafts, headed with a plain cornice. In its general arrangements Bective Abbey differs from every other monastic structure in the kingdom. It is, in fact, a monastic castle, and, previous to the use of artillery, must have been regarded as a place of great strength.

The smaller churches of the close of the twelfth, and of the early half of the thirteenth century, are not different in general form from those of an earlier age. In a few examples, indeed, transepts occur, as in the church of Clady, adjoining Bective, but they are not invariably evidences of comparatively recent work, being sometimes found in connexion with very early churches to which they have evidently been added, and from which, in their architectural details, they differ in every respect.

Down to the very latest period of pointed architecture the original plan of a simple nave, or nave and chancel, was followed; and the chief or only difference observable in churches of very early date, from those of the sixth and seventh centuries, consists in the form of the arch-heads, the position of the doorway, the style of the masonry, which is usually much better in the more ancient examples, and the use of bell-turrets, the *Cloigtheach* or detached round towers having answered this purpose during the earlier ages.

Choir Arch of Cannistown Church, near Navan, Co. Meath.

A beautiful and highly characteristic example of an early pointed church may be seen at Cannistown, not far from Bective, upon the opposite side of the Boyne. As usual it consists of nave and chancel, and there are the remains of a bell-turret upon the west gable, the usual position. The choir arch is represented in the annexed cut. There are numerous instances of churches in this style scattered over the entire island, but they are usually plain, and the choir arch is generally the least adorned feature of the building.

As examples the reader is referred to the churches

of Kilbarrack, Dalkey, Kinsaly, and Rathmichael, all
in the immediate neighbourhood of Dublin. The
church at Dalkey indeed cannot be regarded as a
first-rate example, as it has evidently been altered
and remodelled at various times. A portion of
its northern nave wall, including the semicircularly
arched window, may probably have formed part of an
extremely ancient *teampull*, dedicated to St. Begnet,
which is recorded to have stood here. It may be
observed that the piscinas, or stoups, do not occur in
the early churches of Ireland; they appear to have
been adopted during the latter half of the twelfth
century, and churches of a later period frequently
contain several.

The church of St. Doulough, the origin of which is
involved in the deepest obscurity, is the most remarkable and unique example of pointed architecture remaining in Ireland. It stands at a distance of about
four miles from Dublin, in the direction of Malahide,
and has long occupied the attention of writers upon the
subject of Irish antiquities. This church has generally
been classed with the stone-roofed chapels and oratories of the early Irish saints; but in style it differs
completely from those buildings; and numerous architectural peculiarities, evidently original, prove the
structure to belong to the latter end of the thirteenth
century. In plan it is an oblong, with a low square
tower in the centre. A projection on the southern
wall of the tower contains a passage leading from the
lower part of the building to an exceedingly small

chamber, in the eastern wall of which are two windows,
one commanding the only entrance to the church, the
other an altar in an apartment or chapel between the
tower and the west gable. The body of structure
is divided upon the interior by a mass of masonry
which was evidently intended to support the roof, and
which contains a small semicircular arch now stopped
up. The western apartment measures 10 by 7½ feet;
it is vaulted, and was anciently lighted by several
windows with flat or trefoiled heads. The altar, or
" tomb," as it is popularly called, rests immediately
against the masonry which divides this apartment from
other portions of the building. The chapel or eastern
division measures 21 by 9½ feet. It was lighted by
four windows, one to the east, two to the south, and
one, now stopped up, to the north. The eastern window
is larger than the others, and is divided into two lights
by a shaft, with shallow hollows at the sides and a
semi-cylindrical moulding on its external face. Similar
hollows, and a moulding, run round the arch, and meet
those of the shafts. The northern window is of plain
early lancet form. The windows in the southern wall
are unequal in size; the larger one is placed beneath
the tower, near the centre of the building, and is
divided by a shaft into two lights, the heads of which
are cinque-foiled, while the space between them and
the crown of the arch is left plain. The vaults of the
lower apartments form the floor of a croft occupying
uninterruptedly the whole length of the church. There
are the remains of a fireplace in the centre of the

northern wall of this singular room, which appears to
have been used anciently as a habitation. It is lighted
by small tre-foiled opes in the end walls, and is higher
by several feet, for a distance of about four yards from

St. Doulough's Church, Co. Dublin.

the west gable, than in the other part. By this
arrangement, and by a depression of the vault of the
western division of the building, provision is made for
a small intermediate chamber to which a passage from
the tower leads. The latter was divided by a wooden

floor into two stories, the lower of which contains a
small fireplace.   The roof is formed of stones, well cut,
and laid in regular courses. It has been suggested that
the tower is more modern than the church; its upper
portion is certainly different in style of masonry from
the rest of the building, and appears to be an addition
or restoration; but the body of the tower is clearly
coeval with the church.

Such are the more remarkable features of this singular and unexampled structure, in the erection of
which the architect appears studiously to have avoided
every principle of so-called Gothic composition except
variety.

St. Doulough's Well.

The well of St. Doulough, which was probably also
used as a baptistry, is quite in keeping with the curious
character of the church.   The spring, which is covered
by a stone-roofed octagonal building, rises through a
circular basin, cut out of a single stone, and was not
many years ago thought to possess miraculous powers.
According to tradition the interior was anciently

decorated with pictures, and holes are pointed out as having been made for the reception of iron pins, or holdfasts, by which they were secured to the wall.

Adjoining is a most curious subterranean bath. It is supplied by the well; and even yet the water rises to a considerable depth within it. According to D'Alton the well was dedicated to the Blessed Virgin, and the bath was called "St. Catherine's Pond."

St. Doulough's, the castle and church of Malahide, the church of Howth (generally styled "The Abbey"), the grand cromleac in Lord Howth's demesne, which beautiful locality is free to the public on Saturday, and after the hours of Church Service on Sundays; and the church of St. Fenton, or Fintan, on Howth, might each and all be visited in one day. Howth is within a short railway distance from Dublin, and several trains pass daily to and fro. The "abbey" church of Howth stands near the edge of a cliff, the base of which was formerly washed by the sea. It owes its origin to an ancestor of the present Lord Howth, and was erected in the early part of the thirteenth century. Placed upon a precipitous bank, considerably elevated above the water's edge, and surrounded by a strong embattled wall, it presents a striking evidence of the half-monk, half-soldier, character of its founders. A considerable portion of the original structure remains, but the whole of the north side is comparatively late. The porch, in connexion with the southern doorway, is a very unusual feature in churches found in Ireland—a fact not easily to be accounted for, as they appear to have

been common in England during mediæval times.
The nave arches, which are of the pointed form, are
six in number ; and with the exception of the two
adjoining the eastern end, which are separated by
an octagonal pillar, they spring from rudely-formed
quadrangular piers. A bell turret with three apertures rises from the western gable ; the bells are
said to be preserved in the castle.

The tomb of Christopher, the twentieth Lord of
Howth, who died in 1580, stands in the nave not
far from the eastern gable. It is a nice specimen
of the altar-tomb, but an inscription which it bears,
owing to the neglected state in which the monument, until lately, was suffered to lie, has become
illegible.

The little church of St. Fenton, or Fintan, situated
upon the Hill of Howth, not far from the village of
Sutton, cannot be of earlier date than " The Abbey."
This singular building measures upon the interior but
16½ feet in length, by 7 feet 8 inches in breadth, yet
it contains five windows : one to the east, two to the
south, one to the north, and one in the west gable.
These opes are of various forms : that to the east has
a semicircular head with a multifoil moulding ; one
of the windows in the south-side wall is covered with
a single stone, out of which a semicircular arch-head
is cut, while the other is quadrangular. All the
windows splay widely upon the interior. A doorway in the lancet form is placed in the western gable,
which supports a bell-turret of considerable dimensions,

and strangely out of proportion to the size of the structure. It contains one small pointed aperture for the reception of a bell.

Of the origin of this church absolutely nothing is known; but its date is sufficiently indicated by various architectural peculiarities which it exhibits, and which are characteristic of the close of the thirteenth, or early part of the fourteenth century. The cromleac of Howth, lies not far from St. Fintan's, in a north-easterly direction. It stands within the demesne, which is only open to visitors on Saturdays, and on Sundays after the hours of mid-day service in the Protestant church (see p. 65). Such of my readers as may be induced to visit the locality will find in its antiquities much subject for study and observation.

Students of archæology should not fail to examine the extremely ancient church remaining on Ireland's Eye, a romantic islet, or rock, in the immediate vicinity of the harbour. The place was formerly known as *Inis-mac-Nessan*, from the three sons of Nessan, viz. Dicholla, Munissa, and Nadsluagh, who some time in the seventh century erected the little *teampull* or *cill*, much of which still remains. An arch spanning its eastern end formerly sustained a round tower belfry, the base of which can even now be traced.

CHAPTER II.

FONTS.

CHARACTER OF THE EARLY FONTS—EXAMPLES AT KILLINEY AND
KILTERNAN—FONTS AT KILCARN, CO. MEATH; ST. JOHN'S POINT,
CO. DOWN; KILLESHIN, CO. CARLOW; DUNSANY, CO. MEATH;
ARMAGH.

VERY considerable number of ancient baptismal fonts still remain within the walls
of the ruined churches of Ireland, and
others are found in graveyards where churches, of
which no vestige remains, formerly stood. The fonts
usually found in connexion with the more ancient
churches are extremely rude, and of small dimensions,
being rarely large enough to allow of the immersion of
infants. They are almost in every instance formed of
a single stone, clumsily hollowed, and having a hole at
the bottom of the basin; but in some instances no mode
of escape for the water appears.

An extremely early font occurs in the ancient church
of Killiney, Co. Dublin, and there is another in the
equally ancient church of Kilternan, not far from
Foxrock railway station on the Dublin and Bray
line. An example, in which there is no passage by

which the water can be allowed to escape, may be seen in the church of St. John's Point, Co. Down. The earliest fonts are generally somewhat circular in form, but the stone appears only to have been roughly hammered, and in no instance can be perceived any attempt at decoration ; perhaps the oldest ornamented font remaining in Ireland is that which stands in the graveyard of Killeshin. It is of a bulbous form, and the base is cut into an octagon figure. After the twelfth century fonts of greater size, and supported by a short column, appear to have become common. Their form is generally octagonal, but they are seldom enriched in any way, and when ornaments occur they consist only of a few mouldings upon the shafts or upon the upper edge of the basin. From the absence of mouldings in the majority of instances, it is extremely difficult to assign a date to the numerous fonts of an octagon form which remain in many parts of the country. During the period of debased Gothic architecture, a great many appear to have been erected in Ireland, particularly in the district comprising the old English Pale. We have engraved an unusually fine example from the mediæval church of Kilcarn, near Navan, in the county of Meath. Placed upon its shaft, as represented in the cut, it measures in height about 3 feet 6 inches; the basin is 2 feet 10 inches in diameter, and 13 inches deep. The heads of the niches, twelve in number, with which its sides are carved, are enriched with foliage of a graceful, but uniform character ; and the miniature buttresses which separate the niches are decorated with crockets, the bases

Font of Kilcarn, Co. Meath.

resting upon heads, grotesque animals, or human figures, carved as brackets. The figures within the niches are executed with a wonderful degree of care, the drapery being represented with each minute crease or fold well expressed. They were evidently intended to represent Christ, the Virgin Mary, and the twelve Apostles. All the figures are seated. Our Saviour, crowned as a King, holding in His hand the globe and cross, is in the act of blessing the Virgin, who is also crowned, the "Queen of Heaven." The figures of most of the Apostles can be easily identified : St. Peter, by his key ; St. Andrew by his cross of

Font of Kilcarn. No. 1.

peculiar shape ; and so on. They are represented barefooted, and each holds a book in one hand. The font does not now rest upon its ancient shaft, nor has it done so, in the memory of the old people of the neighbouring villages, but the shaft still remains within the church, and the whole might be easily restored. Since the above was written, this interesting monument has been removed to the Roman Catholic Church of Johnstown, immediately adjoining.

Font of Kilcarn.   No. 2.

A font almost precisely similar in design may be seen in the choir of the ruined church of Dunsany, near Dunshaughlin, in the same county, but it is of smaller size, and the figures and ornaments with which it is sculptured are less prominent than those upon the example at Kilcarn. A fine and unusually large font remains in Christ Church

Font of Kilcarn.   No. 3.

Font of Kilcarn.   No. 4.

Cathedral, Dublin, and in several churches, to which I have referred the reader, interesting specimens occur.

Just about forty-nine years ago the grand Cathedral
Church of Armagh contained a baptismal font which
has been described as covered with the figures of angels
and other sacred emblems. At that time the venerable
structure had been handed over to an English architect,
named Cottingham, for the purpose of being by him
thoroughly restored. The original Cathedral certainly
still stands, but no person of the present generation, at
least, has ever seen it, the "restorer" having veneered
the whole of its outer walls, tower, and all with thin
sandstone flags!* The interior is almost equally ob-
scured by plastering. But this is not all. As stated
by Mr. Edward Rogers in his interesting "Memoir
of Armagh Cathedral," Mr. Cottingham "sent the
font to London, and from it was designed the present
mediæval one. The original stone, however, was
retained to enhance the stock of Mr. Cottingham's
museum, and at his death was sold for a high figure."
This was restoration indeed! Armagh Cathedral was
taken in hands at least forty years too soon. But even
in our own day not a few fantastic tricks have been
performed in the way of conservation.

* "The Screen" of this Cathedral, wrote Dr. Petrie, "is indeed
beautiful in its way, but in a way we never had in Ireland. The
restorer of the Cathedral should be an Irish historical architect and
antiquary. This Mr. Cottingham was not."

CHAPTER III.

CASTLES.

MALAHIDE—TRIM—SCURLOUGHSTOWN—BULLOCK.

THOUGH the castles of Ireland, in point of architectural magnificence, are not to be compared with some of the more important structures of a similar character in England, they are frequently of very considerable extent. Placed as they generally are upon the summit of a lofty and precipitous rock, the base of which is usually washed by the waters of a river or lake, or by the sea, encompassed with walls and towers pierced with shot-holes, and only to be approached through well defended gateways, they must, before the introduction of artillery, have been generally considered impregnable. Several of the early keeps are circular, but they usually consist of a massive quadrangular tower with smaller towers at the angles. The internal arrangements are similar in character to those observable in the military structures of the same period in England and elsewhere. The outworks and other appendages to the majority of our most remarkable castles have been destroyed, not by the usual effects of time and neglect, but by gunpowder, as the enormous masses of masonry overthrown, lying in confused heaps, sufficiently testify. The cannon of Cromwell left almost every stronghold of the Irish and of the Anglo-Irish in ruins. Shortly after the Restoration the necessity for castles ceased, and, with some exceptions, the few that had escaped the violence of the preceding period appear gradually to have been deserted and suffered to decay.

Malahide Castle, Co. Dublin.

The castle of Malahide, situated within a journey of half-an-hour by railway from Dublin, is perhaps the most perfectly preserved of the ancient baronial residences now remaining in Ireland. It owes its foundation to Richard Talbot, who, in the reign of King Henry II., received a grant of the lordship of Malahide, and from whom the present lord is a lineal descendant. The castle, upon the exterior, retains but little of its ancient character; portions have been rebuilt; the old loopholes have given place to modern windows; the tower upon the south-east angle is an addition of the present century; the formidable out-works have long been removed and a grassy hollow indicates the position of the ancient moat; yet not-withstanding all these changes it is still an object of great antiquarian interest. The engraving represents the castle from the south-west angle. You enter through a low "Gothic" porch, attached to which is the ancient oaken door studded with huge nails, and from which the original knocker is suspended. The interior presents many features unique in Ireland. The celebrated oak room with its quaintly carved arabesques, black as ebony, the antique and beautiful armour with which it is appropriately decorated, and the storied panels of its northern side form altogether a scene worthy the description of a Scott or the pencil of a Roberts. Several of the other apartments are well worthy of examination, particularly the banqueting hall, a room of noble proportions and retaining its original oaken roof. The walls of the chief rooms are hung with pictures and portraits, several of which are of great historical interest. Among the former an altar-piece by Albert Durer is perhaps the most remarkable. It is divided into compartments representing the Nativity, Adoration, and Circumcision. This inte-resting picture, which is said to have belonged to Queen Mary of Scotland, was purchased by Charles II. for the sum of £2000, and presented by him to the Duchess of Portland, who gave it to the grand-mother of the late Colonel Talbot. The portraits are

chiefly by Vandyke, Sir Peter Lely, and Sir Godfrey
Kneller. Those of Charles I. and Henrietta Maria,
by Vandyke, are noble examples of that great master's
power.

The chapel, popularly called the "Abbey" of Malahide,
lies a little to the east of the castle. Though its architectural features are no way remarkable, it is a building
of great picturesque beauty. The *perpendicular* window
in the east end, however, should be seen, as also the
tomb of Maud Plunkett, lying in the nave. Of this
lady it is recorded that she was a maid, wife, and
widow in one day, her husband having fallen when
resisting a sudden predatory attack made by a neighbouring clan during the day of his marriage. The
story forms the subject of a beautiful ballad from the
pen of Gerald Griffin.

I have noticed the castle of Malahide first, not that
it is supposed to be the most characteristic example
of an ancient fortress lying within easy access from
Dublin; but because it remains certainly the finest
structure of its age and purpose still inhabited and
occupied by a descendant of the original founder,
at present to be met with in Ireland.*

I shall now refer the reader to a castle of, at
least, equal antiquity, and which, though in a state
of utter ruin, will impress visitors with a much more
correct idea of the ancient feudal stronghold. The

---

* Strangers are admitted to the interior on presenting a card, which
may usually be had on application to his lordship's agent, who resides
in Malahide.

castle of Trim, a town of Meath, upon the borders
of what was once considered "the English Pale"
lies at an easy distance from Dublin, from which
place it may be reached with little delay by rail (see
p. 200).

The late Rev. Richard Butler, in an interesting little
volume entitled "Some Notices of the Castle of Trim,"

Castle of Trim, Co. Meath.

has thrown much light upon the history of this once
formidable stronghold.   From Mr. Butler's book we
have abridged the following description; the original
is from the pen of H. James, Esq., R.E. :—The castle
consists of a triangular walled enclosure, defended by
circular flanking towers, and a large and lofty donjon
or keep in the centre.   The north-eastern side is 171
yards long, and is defended by four towers, viz. two at
the angles, and two intermediate.   The west side is

116 yards long, and was defended by flanking towers
at the angles, and a gateway tower in the centre. The
portcullis groove is very perfect, and it seems, from the
projecting masonry that there had been a drawbridge
and barbican to the gate. The third side sweeps round
at an easy curve to the Boyne; it is 192 yards long,
defended by six flanking towers, including those at the
angles and at the gate. The gate tower is circular and
in good preservation, as well as the arches over the
ditch, and the barbican beyond it. The gate had also
its portcullis, the groove for which, and the recess for
its windlass, are perfect. The circumference of the
castle wall, then, is 486 yards, defended by ten flanking
towers, at nearly equal distances, including those at the
gates. The donjon is a rectangular building, the plan
of which may thus be described :—On the middle of
each side of 64 feet rectangles are constructed, the
sides perpendicular to the square being 20 feet, and
those parallel to it 24 feet : thus a figure of twenty
sides is constructed. The thickness of the walls of the
large tower is 12 feet, and of the smaller towers from
4 feet 6 inches to 6 feet. The walls were carried up
60 feet above the level of the ground, but on each angle
of the large tower square turrets, 16 feet 6 inches in
height are built. By this arrangement, a large shower
of missiles might have been projected in any direction.

A castle, which there is every reason to believe
occupied the site of the present structure, was erected
by Walter de Lacy, who had obtained from Henry II.
a grant of Meath. During the absence of de Lacy,

while the castle was in the custody of Hugh Tyrrell, it was attacked and demolished by Roderick O'Connor, king of Connaught.   In Dr. Hanmer's "Chronicle of Ireland," the circumstance of its erection is thus given:

"Anno 1220.   Meath was wonderfully afflicted and wasted by reason of the private quarrels and civil warres between William, Earl Marshall, Earle of Pembroke, &c., and Sir Hugh de Lacy, Earle of Ulster and Lord of Connaght.   Trimme was besieged and brought to a lamentable plight, and when the rage and fury of those garboiles was somewhat mitigated and appeased, after the shedding of much blood, the same year, to prevent afterclaps and subsequent calamities, the castle of Trim was builded."

The once sumptuous castle of Maynooth, erected in 1176 by Maurice Fitzgerald, can be easily visited from Dublin.   This may be considered a fine example of the kind of structure which combined the baronial residence with the military fortress.   The keep is of the original Norman work.   The ground floor, like that of Athenry Castle, and others of the same period, is divided into two large vaulted apartments over which were state rooms of magnificent proportions. Bedrooms of various sizes occupy the upper portion of the tower.   The servants and members of the household were accommodated in buildings stretching between the barbican of the outworks and a strong flanking tower which still remains.   It is difficult for most visitors to a ruined castle in Ireland to imagine the amount of personal comfort which the old occupiers may have generally enjoyed while dwelling within the now damp and mouldering walls. It is stated in a contemporary account of the sack of this Geraldine stronghold, in the time of Henry VIII., that "great and rich was the spoile, such store of beddes, so many goodly hangings, so rich a wardrob, such brave furniture, as truly it was accompted for householde stuffe and vtensils one of the richest earle his houses under the crowne of Englande."

It seems to have taken a considerable period to reconcile the native Irish to the use of castles or tower houses as places of every-day abode. The free roving Celt could ill brook the confinement of narrow vaults and stifling chambers. To him, as a chieftain actually declared, "a castle of bones was every way preferable to a castle of stones." By this was meant that the head of a clan, surrounded by his following of hardy kerns and gallowglasses was safer, and every way better off than an effeminate sojourner between the four walls of a tower. A time at length arrived when the native potentates, petty chieftains, and gentlemen of less degree, followed the example of their invaders, and erected stone dwellings, very similar to those of the strangers with which they had become familiarized. These almost invariably consist of a tall quadrangular tower, with or without outworks, but generally furnished with a bawn or enclosure into which at night, or during raiding times, the owner's cattle were driven.

The apartment on the ground floor was almost invariably covered with a vault of stone, evidently a precaution against fire. In not a few instances all the flooring was supported on pointed or barrel arches of stone ; but, generally, the upper storeys were provided with floors of timber. A staircase of stone usually led to the upper apartments ; sometimes it ran straight through the thickness of the wall from floor to floor, access to the upper apartments being provided by narrow doorways, with pointed, flat, or semicircular heads. These three forms are not unfrequently found in the one building. Sometimes the staircase is enclosed in a projecting tower, and rises cork-screw fashion, with doorways at one side like those already referred to. A second staircase leading to small apartments, which may have been used as bedrooms, is often to be noticed.

"The entrance to an Irish house, castle, or tower," writes J. H. Parker, c.b., of Oxford (the greatest living authority on the subject of domestic architecture of the middle ages), in whose company it was my fortune to visit a large number of so-called " castles," in various parts of Ireland, " is usually protected in a manner unknown in England—at least not commonly known— for there are a few instances of a similar arrangement in England. There is no external porch, but the door- way opens into a small space, about 6 feet square and about 8 or 10 feet high ; in front is the door to the cellar ; on the right is the door to a small guard- chamber ; on the left the door to the staircase ; each of these doors is barred on the other side, so that the visitor can proceed no further without permission, and

immediately over his head is a small square or round
hole, emphatically called a 'murthering hole'; this
opens into a small chamber in which a pile of paving
stones was kept ready for use, so that if an enemy had
forced the outer door he would not be much the for-
warder. These precautions were evidently taken to
guard against any sudden surprise." But in our Irish
tower-houses there was another provision for security.
The outer doorway was not unfrequently furnished
with a portcullis, so that an unwelcome visitor upon
entering the space referred to by Mr. Parker, with the
doors in front and at the sides fastened, the "murthering hole" above his head, and the portcullis grate
dropped behind him, would be securely entrapped. A
small projecting bartizan or machicolation set in the
top of the tower, is usually found surmounting the
doorway on the exterior. Similar turrets occasionally
protect angles of the building, by means of which
any foe attempting to dislodge the coign stones might
be easily crushed. A large, and often handsomely-
constructed, fireplace is generally found in the principal
apartment. The chimney-shafts, as a rule, are quadrangular. Curiously enough, the kitchen is usually
placed outside the building. In a good many examples
well-constructed " garde-robes," or closets, occur.

The windows, which, it should be observed, are commonly very small, splay internally, and are usually
placed slightly above the level of the floor, from which
they are approached by a few steps. There is generally
a stone seat within the splay, upon each side of the

light. This remark, of course, only refers to the principal opes.

The castle of Scurloughstown, which stood in the immediate vicinity of Trim, was probably as good an example as any which have recently remained of the lesser keep, usually found in those districts wherein the

Scurloughstown Castle.

earlier colonies of the English or Anglo-Normans obtained footing. It no longer exists. The above sketch was made a few years before the tower, which upon one of its sides exhibited a crack extending from summit to foundation, fell to the ground.

The castle of Bullock, standing immediately above the little harbour of the same name, not far from the Dalkey station of the Dublin, Wicklow, and Wexford

Railway, is well worthy of a visit. This, and the neighbouring castles, or tower-houses, of Dalkey, might be reached from Dublin, by rail, in less than half an hour. The latter examples are admirable in their way.

Of the origin of these very interesting structures, no notice, as far as I could ascertain, has been preserved. It is extremely probable that they were erected

Bullock Castle, near Kingstown, Co. Dublin.

by English settlers, not long after the invasion of Ireland, by Strongbow, their architectural features indicating an early period; and similar buildings, connected together by a wall enclosing a very considerable space occurring in several localities known to have been occupied by the old English.

It would be well here to mention the picturesque, and almost perfectly preserved, castle of Drimnagh, lying at a distance of about four miles from Dublin,

on the road to Crumlin. Its bawn is still perfect,
and the ancient fosse, with which the whole was
enclosed, remains in fine preservation, and is still deep.
Drimnagh was considered as a place of considerable
strength during the rising of 1641, and it appears to
have been strengthened, and in a great measure re-
edified, about that unhappy period of Ireland's history.

Pilgrims to the round tower of Swords will find in
its immediate vicinity a fine example of the mediæval
castle and bawn, which formerly belonged to the Archbishops of Dublin. If they return to Dublin by car
they will have an opportunity of inspecting the very
curious church, and well, of St. Doulough, as also
St. Catherine's Pond, adjoining. (See pp. 207, 208,
and 209.)

CHAPTER IV.

TOWN GATES, GATE-TOWERS, AND WALLS,

THE GATES OF DROGHEDA—THE FAIR-GATE AT NEW ROSS, AND OTHERS—ST. AUDOEN'S ARCH, THE LAST REMAINING GATE OF DUBLIN.

LTHOUGH it is pretty certain that the Danes at a very early period encompassed several of the cities and towns which they held in Ireland with ramparts and towers, their works have long disappeared, and though the walls and gates of several of our ancient cities remain, they are obviously of comparatively late date, and invariably found in connexion with places which we know to have been anciently strongholds of the English. Occasionally, as at Drogheda and at Athlone, the wall was of considerable height and thickness. That of Waterford, of which a large portion remains, is strengthened with semicircular towers; but they are usually plain. It is extremely probable that the great majority of these works at present remaining in Ireland were spared simply because since the general application of gunpowder to the purposes of a siege they could no longer be relied upon as fortifications. This much is

certain, that the walls of all the Anglo-Irish cities and
towns, which were anciently remarkable for strength,
and the security they afforded to the besieged, have
been almost entirely destroyed. Several gates and
towers, however, remain, and of these the finest may
be seen at Drogheda.

St. Laurence's Gate, Drogheda.

St. Laurence's Gate, the subject of the annexed
illustration, consists of two lofty circular towers, connected together by a wall, in the lower portion of
which an archway is placed. The towers, as well as
the wall by which they are connected, are pierced with
numerous loop-holes, and it is probable that the latter
was anciently, upon the town side, divided into stages
by platforms of timber, extending from tower to tower,
otherwise the loop-holes could not have been used by

the defenders of the gate; and we know that even in
their most beautiful buildings the ancient architects
rarely added an unnecessary feature.   The other remaining gate-tower of Drogheda is octangular in form,
pierced with long, narrow loop-holes, wider in the
centre than in the other parts, and was further
strengthened by a portcullis, the groove for which

The West Gate, Drogheda.

remains nearly perfect.   The greater number of gate-
towers remaining in Ireland are square, and of considerable height.   Their archways are generally semicircular, but there was a beautiful pointed example at
Ross, in the county of Wexford.   Since the period of
Cromwell's " crowning mercy," the successful storming
of Drogheda, the walls of that place have been gradually
sinking into utter ruin; but, from some portions which

yet remain in a tolerably perfect state, an idea may
be formed of their ancient strength and grandeur.

A view of the "Sheep-gate" of Trim is here presented. The tower by which it was anciently surmounted no longer exists. The wall adjacent seems
to have suffered like denudation. A lofty structure

The Sheep Gate and Yellow Steeple, Trim, Co. Meath.

figured in the distance, the belfry of St. Mary's
Abbey,* is of a late period of Gothic architecture.

The walls and flanking towers of Athenry, in the
county of Galway, are fairly well preserved. Of

---

* Mr. Butler, in his book on the Castle of Trim, remarks that in
1449–50 Richard, Duke of York, held his Court there ; that he was a
benefactor to St. Mary's Abbey ; and that the "yellow steeple," as
the tower is popularly styled, may probably be assigned to his time.

these, a truly fine example of a gate-tower may yet
be seen; though it is no longer used as a port, the
road which passed through it having been diverged to
one side. Will it be believed that this stately relic of
mediæval days was, within the memory of people comparatively young, with difficulty saved from destruction
—a road contractor desiring to have it for the sake
of the material; and that in the stoniest county in
Ireland! Concerning this very structure there was
a tradition amongst the neighbouring people that it
was some time or other to fall upon the wisest man
in Ireland. It will be hardly thought that the greedy
official who coveted the stones need have feared for his
personal safety when passing beneath the arch, for, in
reply to a gentleman who stoutly objected to the pro-
posed removal of the tower, on account of its interesting
antiquity, he is reported to have phoo-phooed, declaring
that any antiquity it ever possessed had gone long ago!

Kilmallock retains two mural gates of considerable
interest. They were very strong, and in times of
need might have served as castles. Galway can
show one fine double bar; and there are others in
Ireland of less import, as those of Londonderry,
which have been all rebuilt within a comparatively
recent period. Dublin citizens, generally, are not
aware that considerable patches of their old walls, including one gate or bar, still remain. The gateway is
called St. Audoen's Arch, and may be seen close to the
ancient church of the same name. It was built by
the citizens during the invasion of Ireland by Edward

Bruce, at a time when he lay encamped at Castleknock and daily threatened the city. The adjoining portion of the wall is here very high and strong ; but the gate-tower has been lowered almost down to its arch. Other portions of the wall, including a tower, may be seen in Ship-street, near the southern entrance to Dublin Castle.

Of the structure originally erected, or rebuilt, by Archbishop Henry de Loundres, A. D. 1220, a considerable portion may possibly be concealed beneath the piles of modern edifices which represent the present Castle of Dublin. It may be said that scarcely a scrap of the original fortress remains visible, and that the " Castle " presents no point of interest whatever to the architectural antiquary.

PART IV.

Miscellaneous Notices.

— ◦◇◦ —

CHAPTER I.

BRIDGES AND CAUSEWAYS.

ANCIENT TIMBER CAUSEWAYS—ANGLO-NORMAN STONE BRIDGES—
OLD THOMOND BRIDGE, LIMERICK—"KEY OF CONNAUGHT"—NEW-
BRIDGE, NEAR LEIXLIP, CO. DUBLIN.

THAT the Irish at an early period were in
the habit of constructing bridges and
causeways over rivers, or from the
mainland to an island, or from one island to another,
is a fact recorded in our Annals; and we are not
wholly without some existing remains of that very
interesting class. We read that in A.D. 1054, a bridge
was built over the Shannon, at Killaloe, by Turlogh
O'Brien. This work was undoubtedly of timber. It
had probably been long decayed or destroyed when
Richard de Clare obtained possession of the greater
part of that county which still bears his name. But
the ford was not so easily obliterated, and Killaloe was
for a considerable time called "Claresford" by the
English. The little island of Begerin, near Wexford,

was formerly connected with another by a causeway, described by Mr. G. H. Kinahan in the *Journal, R. H. A. A. I.*, as consisting of two rows of oak piles, set four feet apart, with about five feet between each pair. " On these piles," he remarks, " there would seem to have originally been longitudinal and transverse beams." St. Ibar, who died in A. D. 500, had a church and monastery in Begerin, so that there is every probability that this bridge, or causeway, may be referred to a very early date. The islands of Devenish and Inismacsaint, in Lough Erne, both of which were monastic sites in the sixth century, had similar communications with the mainland. A number of the piles at the latter-named place may still be seen when the water is low. Several of our lake habitations, or " *crannogs*," were furnished with causeways connecting them with the mainland, or with neighbouring islets.

Few or no bridges formed of stone appear to have been erected in Ireland previous to the Anglo-Norman invasion; but the strangers and their descendants constructed a goodly number, several of which remained down to a comparatively late period. Of these perhaps old Thomond-bridge, which spanned the Shannon at Limerick, was the most remarkable. Low, flat, and narrow in its proportions, defended at one end by a tower and gateway, and exhibiting in its fifteen arches a variety of forms, chiefly of the pointed style of architecture, it constituted, with the castle, and the venerable tower of St. Mary's Abbey in the background, one of a group of mediæval structures as imposing as

picturesque. This work was in all probability coeval
with the castle immediately adjoining, a fortress erected
in the reign of King John. Having at length, in part,
become ruinous it was in the memory of persons still
living pulled down; and a structure more in accordance
with the requirements of the nineteenth century occupies its historic site.

The Shannon, almost in our own time, was crossed
by other bridges of considerable antiquity. That at
Athlone was one of the most interesting and picturesque features of the old town. In its abutments were
recesses intended for the refuge of foot-passengers
whenever any vehicle was passing—a precaution rendered absolutely necessary by the narrow proportions
of the ancient roadway. Near the centre, on the
northern side, might be seen a very remarkable sculptured and inscribed monument, the stones of which
are now in the collection of the Royal Irish Academy.
Why were these not set up in the modern bridge?
But "that new brooms sweep clean" is an old pro-
verb, why, might be further asked, was this ancient
"Key of Connaught," as the bridge was sometimes
called, swept away at all? Why were similar
structures over Ireland's chief rivers, as at Banagher,
and elsewhere, removed? The cost of their destruction exceeded the value of their materials by many
degrees; and for an engineering theory, which turns
out to be baseless, we have lost a goodly number of
monuments often associated with great names and
heroic deeds; and, it may be said, with the idea of

social enterprise or munificence. By the removal of the ancient Shannon bridges, has the winter overflow of the mighty stream been in any manner checked?

Artistic or antiquarian visitors to Dublin should by all means visit Newbridge, near Leixlip, where perhaps the oldest bridge remaining in the United Kingdom may be studied. The trip would occupy, say, less than half a day, and might be almost entirely performed by rail, or steam-tram.

This quaint and venerable structure, which still remains apparently as strong as when it was indeed the *New Bridge*, was, according to Pembridge's Annals, as published by Camden, erected in 1308, by John le Decer, Mayor of Dublin in that year. It is in every respect a most interesting building of its kind, and promises (unless taken in hand by some " restorer ") likely to stand the storms and floods of another five hundred years, and still retain its pristine appearance. Some half century ago the " New Bridge " was sentenced to destruction, as a nuisance, and only escaped demolition through the influence of the then worthy proprietor of St. Woolstan's, Richard Cane, Esq., who, in a spirit worthy of all commendation, declared that he would rather bear the cost of a new bridge than see one stone of John le Decer's work removed.

CHAPTER II.

THE "CRANNOG," OR LAKE HABITATION, AS FOUND IN IRELAND.

LAGORE CRANNOG—"KITCHEN MIDDEN" REMAINS—DRUMKELLIN CRANNOG—MONAGHAN AND FERMANAGH CRANNOGS—CONTINENTAL LAKE DWELLINGS—CRANNOG POTTERY—XYLOGRAPHY—CRANNOG BRONZE SWORD-SHEATHS, SPEARS, SHIELDS—BOATS : THE CURACH.

A PAPER, referring to the great Crannog of Lisnacroghera, county Antrim, read before a meeting of the Royal Historical and Archæological Association of Ireland, on the 6th of August, 1884, I prefaced my communication with certain remarks which, more or less curtailed, are here reproduced.

In many a district through the length and breadth of Erin spreads a desolate moorland, or perhaps a shallow waste of water, affording little or no sign of animal life beyond flocks of plover, the wary snipe, that ancient fisher the heron, or the curlew, whose alarm-note so often wakes the depressing stillness of the locality. Yet it is certain that not a few of these lonely regions were at some long-forgotten time the sites of human society, industry, and even of art of no mean character.

A slight elevation on the surface of a bog, some
bleached sprays of birch, ash, or sallow, or the appearance of a few gray or white stones—reed surrounded,
and rising a few inches above the surface of a loch—
will often to the practised eye indicate the position of
a "*crannog*," by which name "lake habitations" in
Ireland are usually designated. It is, however, to
turf-cutting operations, or to drainage, that the discovery of the great majority of these interesting sites
must be attributed.

Bronze Brooch from Strokestown Crannog.   (Drawn full size.)

"To understand," said Sir William Wilde, in 1851,
who had then paid more attention to the subject of
Irish crannogs than any previous writer on the same
theme, "or appreciate the nature of these dwellings, we
must bring back our minds to the period when the
country around the localities where they occur was
covered with wood, chiefly oak and alder, and when
the state of society had passed from that of the simple
shepherd, or pastoral condition, to one of rapine,
plunder, and invasion. Certain communities, families,
or chieftains required greater security for themselves,

their cattle, or their valuables, than the land could afford, and so betook themselves to the water. With infinite labour, considering the means and appliances at their disposal, these people cut down young oak-trees, which they carried to the lakes and drove into the clay or mud around the shallows of these islands, which were usually, I believe, covered with water in winter; and having thus formed a stockade which rose above the water into a breastwork, probably interlaced with saplings, they floored with alder, sallow, or birch, to a suitable height above the winter flood the space so enclosed, and on this platform erected wooden cabins. One large flag, at least, was also carried in for a hearthstone, or common cooking-place; and one or more querns, or hand-mills, have almost invariably been found in the remains of these crannogs."

The first crannog brought to light, at least in modern days, seems to have been that of Lagore, near Dunshaughlin, Co. Meath. This occurred about 1844. A few years subsequently the attention of archæologists was attracted by several similar discoveries in Switzerland and Savoy. It is a curious consideration that to water, so usually held inimical to the duration of works constructed of wood, we, as well as many of our Continental friends, owe the preservation of some of the most ancient and interesting of our primitive dwellings. Since the discovery at Lagore, from time to time in various parts of Ireland, in Scotland, and even in England, as well as upon the Continent, lacustrine retreats have been found, and more or less, with their contents, described. Those in this country already recognized number upwards of a hundred and ninety-eight. Some of them were of very considerable dimensions, and contained the remains of several huts. Others are of surprisingly small proportions, and capable of holding but one poor dwelling. All, however, were strongly stockaded, and were fairly secure retreats for their occupiers, who, no doubt, would have managed that no boat or *curach*, excepting those which they had with them upon the island, remained in the neighbourhood.

The larger crannogs, like those of Ballinderry, Westmeath ; Lagore, Co. Meath ; and Lough Gur, Co. Limerick, were undoubtedly fortresses differing in no manner except in position from the dun or rath of *terra firma*. Their " kitchen middens" when examined bring forth exactly the same class of ancient remains, stone, flint, bronze, iron, bone, wood, and even glass. A peculiarity of the " finds" in connexion with the greater islands is the enormous quantity of animal remains, often amounting to hundreds of tons, with which the stockades are found surrounded. These usually consist of the bones of the *bos longifrons* and *bos frontosis*, of the *cervus elephus*, or red deer, wild boars, horses, asses, sheep, foxes, wolf-dogs, and even of human beings. Intermixed with the osseous *débris* very frequently occur innumerable articles of early manufacture, pottery, swords, spear-heads, battle-axes, knives, chains and fetters, spears, reaping-hooks, saws, gouges, brooches, whorls, small frying-pans and pots, horse furniture, crucibles, beads, combs, tweezers, and even pins and needles.

Perhaps, the oldest instance of a wooden hut ever discovered in Europe is one described many years ago by Captain Mudge, R. N., in the " Archæologia." It lay 14 feet beneath the surface of a bog at Drumkellin, Co. Donegal ; and within it was found a stone hatchet, the cutting edge of which is said to have exactly fitted certain indentations which were observable in several of its timbers, all of which were of oak. This structure was perfectly square in plan, 12 feet in each side, and 9 feet high. It was divided on the interior by a flooring into an upper and lower chamber, which were probably only used as sleeping apartments. At the time of the discovery nothing was known about crannogs, and no search was made for the piling with which it was in all likelihood environed. The work was supposed to stand alone. The remains at Dunshaughlin, or more correctly, Lagore crannog, though probably of later date than the building noticed by Captain Mudge, were very similar to it in character ; they, however, presented no upper chamber. The plan of the huts (there were probably six or eight originally) I am able to describe from personal observation made in the summer of 1848, at which time a portion of the " island " was re-opened for the purpose of turf-cutting. Let the reader imagine a foundation consisting of four rough planks of oak, each about 12 feet in length, so arranged as to form a quadrangle. The ends are carefully fitted together, and secured by strong iron nails, with flat heads about the size of a shilling. From the angles of this square rise four posts to the height of about 9 feet. In these grooves are cut, into which roughly split planks of oak have been slipped, so as to form the sides of the dwelling. There seems to have been no provision for the admission of air or light, except a small opening in one of the sides which must have served as a doorway. The roofs were, like the sides, formed of oaken boards—were quite flat, but may, anciently, have been covered with scraws or vegetable matter. The enclosing circles of piles or " hedges," as they were sometimes styled, at Lagore, had been all but completely obliterated before any antiquary had visited the place. Nevertheless, down to the period of my first visit some traces remained. These consisted of half-burnt beams, intermixed with large quantities of wood-charcoal. We gather from history that Lagore once stood one of the strongest and, as there is reason to believe, richest of the island habitations of Ireland. It belonged, in fact, to the O'Melaghlins, a regal family in Meath, and was probably their principal strength. Upon this place the Danes of Dublin had long set their eyes, but had never been able to place their feet, until mustering an army, and carrying with them from Dublin Bay one of their war vessels, they were able, by aid of the latter, to take and sack the crannog. This was in the ninth century.

It is not for a moment to be supposed that all crannogs belong, as a rule, to nearly the above-named period. Some are unquestionably of much

earlier date, while we possess the clearest historical
evidence that others, if not previously constructed,
were used in the fifteenth, and even sixteenth centuries, and even later.   In not a few have been
found cores, accompanied by flakes, scrapers, knives,
arrow-heads, &c., &c., the material of which is flint.
With them sometimes occurred axe-heads of stone,
usually styled "celts," exactly similar to examples
found in primitive cists, along with burial urns
and evidences of cremation.   No doubt flint and
worked stone-bearing crannogs should be regarded
as the oldest, and yet from the fact of spear-heads,
celts, and other articles of early bronze, and of iron
being at times found plentifully amongst their piling,
or in the surrounding bog stuff, we must conclude
that these islets had been used by a people well
skilled in the art of metallurgy.   It should be observed that almost season after season evidence is
produced to indicate that in Ireland at least the contemporaneous adoption of flint, stone, bone, and iron in the
manufacture of weapons, implements, and ornaments
for the person, had existed for a period to be counted
by tens of centuries.   In a Monaghan crannog, described
by Mr. Shirley, stone celts, a worked flint apparently
intended for an arrow-head, three bronze celts with
loops at their sides, a dagger and chisel of bronze, as
also two bronze arrow-heads and a shield-boss of the
same metal were found, accompanied by iron remains.
At a place named "The Miracles," near Monea, Co.
Fermanagh, about fifteen years ago an artificial island,

the remains of which I had an opportunity of examining, was discovered by turf-cutters. Here a beautifully polished axe-head, chisel, or handstone celt was turned up, together with a number of articles composed of bronze which, from the description of the people who had found them as given to me, were probably fibulæ. That during some portion of the period of its occupation inhabitants of this crannog were in the habit of manufacturing objects of iron is quite certain, as pieces of iron slag, quantities of wood charcoal, a well-formed crucible, sharpening stones, and at least two grinding-stones were found amongst the *débris*. In the nearly drained site of Loughavilly ("the Loch of the ancient tree"), near Toppid Mountain, Co. Fermanagh, are the remains of a piled mound, formerly an island. Here, I myself picked up a stone celt and lumps of iron slag. Traces of charcoal were abundant, but from the softness of the surroundings it seemed quite hopeless to penetrate to any extent into the mud or pulp in quest of discoveries.

It may be stated, in short, that in nearly every crannog hitherto discovered, and more or less explored, in Ireland, articles formed of flint or stone, and similar in every respect to remains usually assumed to belong to the so-called "Stone Age," have occurred, and very frequently in apparent connexion with implements of bronze and iron. The manner in which stone celts, discovered in our crannogs, were used, remains to be determined. Certain it is that the long straight clean cuts which invariably appear on the ends of the pilings or stakes by which the islands are environed, could only have been made with the aid of extremely sharp metallic instruments of the axe or adze kind. Such objects are very common in crannog "finds"; and, it should be observed, not a few are furnished with well-steeled cutting edges, while the remainder of the head consists of soft iron. The mortice-holes so often found in the framework of the islets, and in the larger timbers of the huts, were evidently worked out by the use of metal chisels, which may have been formed either of bronze or iron.

It would be impossible, in the space assigned to this handbook, to more than glance at the general features of these curious retreats as found in Erin, and to describe a few of the more characteristic of their contents.

However, without incurring any danger of being considered over-excursive, I may state that in several Swiss lakes, as well as elsewhere upon the continent of Europe, structures every way identical with some of our crannogs have been long noticed and described—I allude to artificial islands, composed mainly of stone, with piles driven into the soil round the water's edge to prevent the mass from slipping. "Still, in the main," writes Mr. John Stewart, Secretary to the Society of Antiquaries of Scotland, "the use of piles in Switzerland was for the purpose of sustaining large platforms upon which whole villages were erected." We appear to have possessed no works of this kind in Ireland, but clusters of crannogs, as in Lough Eyes,

Co. Fermanagh, sometimes occur, and were, as is evident from existing remains, connected together by causeways, or bridges of timber supported high and dry on piles.

Crannog Pottery, &c. — As has been already stated, the contents of our crannogs generally comprise pottery, and objects composed of flint, stone, bronze, iron, glass, and wood, respectively. Bracelets and beads of jet, and combs of bone, are not of unfrequent

Crannog Comb. (Full size.)

occurrence. Ornaments or other articles formed of gold or silver have hardly ever been found even in our richest crannogs; and, strange as it may appear, there is a total absence of the "circulating medium" other than coins of very late date, those issued from the mints of James the Second, when he melted much of his artillery to produce the celebrated "gun money," being the most common. Such cash had probably belonged to banished men, or "*rapparees*," who after the downfall of the Stuart cause were compelled to live in places difficult of access, and had sought the ancient crannogs as exceptionably safe retreats.

But it is not on the subject of comparatively modern
or even mediæval renderings from our lake habitations
I would now treat. To the long mysterious past, to
characteristic examples of the handiwork of people
who perhaps more than a thousand years ago held the
country now called Ireland, and who in all probability
lived and toiled on our crannog sites, I shall at present
venture, as far as considerations of space permit, to
draw the reader's attention.

Fig. 1.—Cooking Vessel from a Crannog in Lough Eyes, Co. Fermanagh.

Amongst the antiquities referred to, perhaps certain
remains of pottery which had evidently been used for
cooking purposes will, by many antiquaries, be considered of very high interest. Figs. 1 and 2 represent
a couple of these vessels from Lough Eyes, county of
Fermanagh. The first measures 8 inches in height

by the same in breadth at the mouth; the second is
6 inches larger in every way. Some of these remains
are considerably smaller. The ornament which they
usually bear is a chevron, such as is often found upon
fictile ware discovered in sepulchral tumuli, as well as
upon several varieties of bronze celts and other weapons
or instruments of, with us, prehistoric times.

Fig. 2.—Cooking Vessel from Lough Eyes, Co. Fermanagh.

In not one single instance on crannog pottery has
there been discovered a trace of what might be called
Christian art or design. All the earthen vessels of
this class hitherto found were hand-made, and appear
to have been well burnt; they are invariably unglazed.
It is a curious circumstance that in many examples the

action of fire would seem to have been more intense
internally than on the exterior. The material is invariably sandy clay ; possibly the grit was added in
order to afford greater consistence to the paste. Most
of the vases show this sand distinctly, and in the ruder
specimens particles of white stone, occasionally the size
of a small pea, and sometimes no bigger than the head

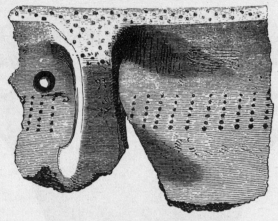

Fragment of Cooking Vessel from Lough Eyes, showing provision for the
escape of steam.

of a pin, may be noticed roughly projecting from their
sides. A number of flat discs of the same material as
the vessels were found with them, and would seem to
have been their covers or lids. A curious provision for
the escape of steam during the process of boiling or cooking is observable in some of these earthen *pots*. It consists of a small circular aperture in the neck, or upper side
of the vessel, just below the point where the lid would
be supported or caught. It is not possible to determine

whether these vessels, when entire, were invariably perforated or otherwise; the aperture, however, occurs in not a few of the specimens preserved. It should be mentioned that the colour of this ware varies from light drab to extremely dark brown. A few, indeed, are slightly red in appearance. Curiously enough, vessels of the same shape and exact style of ornamentation appear to be unknown in every part of the world, with the exception of some districts of North America, where they are discovered in Indian burial mounds of remote but unascertained date.

The principal sources of this pottery in Ireland were the crannogs of Ballydoolough, Drumgay, Lough Eyes, Drumdarragh, and Lankhill, all in the county of Fermanagh; but valuable specimens have been found at Lisnacroghera, and other places. The late Sir W. R. Wilde, when compiling his " Catalogue of Antiquities," preserved in the Museum of the Royal Irish Academy, did not know of the existence of this curious ware.

Xylography, or the art of engraving designs on wood, was largely practised by the ancient Irish. We know that they possessed plenty of timber, and were wonderful adepts at manufacturing " *methers*," or " *madders*," and other household vessels, principally out of alder, oak, and yew. An example, somewhat recently found within the bounds of a crannog-bearing bog on Toppid Mountain, Co. Fermanagh, is here given. The material is oak. It possessed an ornamented cover or lid which has unfortunately been lost. Mr. Bernard Bannon, of Cavancarragh, was the

first to recognize the importance of this beautiful
" find."

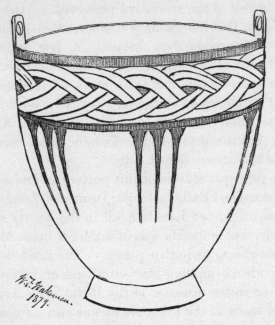

Engraved Oaken Vessel from Toppid Mountain, Co. Fermanagh.   The shading
indicates spaces slightly sunk, and filled with black colouring matter.

Crannog Swords.—The swords discovered in our
lake dwellings are extremely various in character, but
they are all strikingly Celtic.   A few have been
formed of bronze, and differ in no respect from
the greater number of their fellows unearthed in
districts where, apparently, crannogs were not used.
The immense majority are of iron, and are remarkable as a rule for their comparatively small size—
their handles particularly so : hence it has been

inferred that the race or races by whom they were
used must have been diminutive people. But the
same remark may be applied to nearly all the swords
of antiquity of which we know anything.   In shape
they may be described, generally, as of two kinds—
the one increasing in breadth from the handle to the
end, which terminates in the form of a triangle ; the
other is shorter, with a broad blade, quite in the
Roman fashion.   Both are double edged, and are
usually strengthened by a central ridge, while some
rare examples are fluted. Their handles were for the
most part composed of bone or horn, though sometimes
wood was used, and were, as a rule, finished by a
pommel, or knob of a semicircular or triangular
form, secured and strengthened on the inner side by
a plate of bronze, curving backwards.   There is no
hilt or guard, properly speaking, though the haft or
handle usually somewhat overlaps the sides and edges
of the blade, presenting a crescent-like figure, the
curve of which tends in a direction opposite to that
of the pommel.   Bronze mountings frequently occur.
Through the kindness of the Committee of the Royal
Society of Antiquaries of Ireland, I am enabled here
to reproduce illustrations, which appeared in their
Journal, of several bronze sheaths which were found
at Lisnacroghera, in connexion with, at least, three
swords of the crannog class. Very few remains of
the kind have been discovered in Ireland. Wilde, in
his " Catalogue," could not point to a single specimen. He, however, notices some small, undecorated

objects, composed of bronze, little bigger than a
lady's scissors-case, which, in all probability, were the
sheaths of small knives or skeans.   At Lisnacroghera,

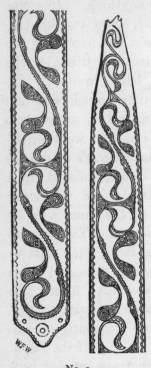

four superb examples, very
nearly perfect, of sword-
sheaths, of bronze, which had
certainly contained iron blades,
have, within the last few years,
been brought to light; some
portions of at least four others
also occurred in the same place.
"Kemble, in his *Horæ Ferales*,"
as remarked by the late Rev.
James Graves, " illustrates several short swords or daggers,
the fashion of which is identical with that now, for the
first time, so clearly shown us
by the Lisnacroghera find."
Illustrations which Kemble
presents* show both sides of a
sword and sheath, and their

No. 1.

Upper and Lower Portions of
Sword-sheath of Bronze, from
Canon Grainger's Lisnacro-
ghera Collection.

likeness to our Ulster examples is most striking: the
haft of the sword is of a
similar character, and the

ends of the bronze sheaths identical.

This relic had been discovered in the river Witham,
in England.   The bed of the Thames has, from

* *Horæ Ferales*, Kemble, p. 182, pl. xvii., fig. 2.

time to time, presented examples equally interesting.

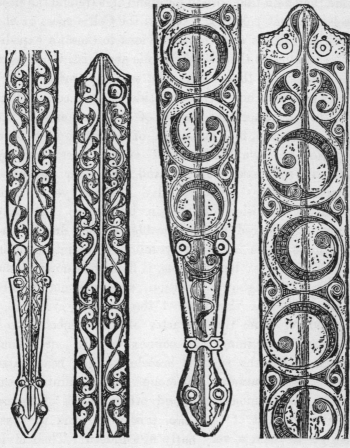

No. 2.

Upper and Lower Portions of
Sword-sheath of Bronze from
Lisnacroghera. Now in the
British Museum.

No. 3.

Upper and Lower Portions of Sword-
sheath of Bronze from Lisnacroghera.
Now in Canon Grainger's Collection.

"Kemble's editors," wrote Mr. Graves, "are inclined

to fix the date of these weapons about the year 100 B.C.;
and they hold that both in England and Ireland the close
relation that subsisted between the Celtic races of the
British Islands and Gaul, previous to Cæsar's expedi-
tions, indicates that the Britannic and Irish Celts were
not far behind their continental contemporaries."

It need not, however, be considered quite certain that
the Lisnacroghera sheaths are of a date anterior to the
first century A. D.   The spirit of Celtic art in Britain
appears to have been almost entirely destroyed by
Roman influence.   In Ireland its career remained
unassailed for, probably, five hundred years later
than the invasion of Britain by Cæsar.   It may
have experienced a considerable change during the
centuries which immediately followed the introduction
of Christianity ; but, with us, it flourished down to the
time of Strongbow's invasion, and was not wholly
extinct even in the days of the Stuarts.

Judging from the character of some objects found
apparently in immediate connexion with our Lisnacroghera sheaths, such as bracelets of jet, beads, axe-
heads, and hammers of stone, worked flints, spear
butts, sword mountings, and other articles of bronze
similar to that of the celts, paalstaves, &c., we must
assign to them a very early age indeed.   Their style
of ornamentation, it should be observed, is completely
free from Byzantine and later ideas—is truly Celtic,
and "racy of the soil."

Sheaths of bronze, wonderfully like our Irish examples, and containing blades of iron, have been

found on the Continent at La Tène. See "Lake Dwellings of Europe," by Robert Munro, M.A., M.D. (Cassell & Co.).

Crannog Spears, &c.—Very few spear-heads of bronze have been noticed in our lake dwellings, while arms of that class—javelins and arrow-heads composed of iron—are extremely numerous. As may be judged from examples found at Lisna-croghera, the spear-shaft was usually about 8 feet in length; but one specimen, now in the Museum of Canon Grainger, has, as far I am aware, been completely preserved. It is of ash. Objects of antique bronze, exactly in the form of a modern door-handle, may be seen in almost every important collection of Irish antiquities. Up to a recent period they constituted a perfect puzzle to archæologists. That they were the butt-ends of spear-shafts is now certain. Indeed, at Lisnacroghera a couple were found still retaining within them the end of the handle. The mode in which they had been attached to the shaft is thus described by Canon Greenwell, who had secured at least five specimens from that crannog:—"The end of the shaft is split, and into the split is inserted a wedge of wood, so that when driven home the wedge expanded the end of the shaft, and kept it firm in the butt."

Butt-end of Crannog Spear-shaft. From Canon Grainger's Collection.

The iron spear-heads are often very elegant in form, and in not a few instances their sockets are ornamented with chevron and other tasteful patterns. They were secured to the handle by bronze ferrules, or by rivets of the same metal, or of iron, which sometimes projected beyond the sides of the shaft, as we see depicted in Anglo-Saxon manuscript drawings. The ferrules occasionally exhibit depressions or scorings which would seem to have been intended for the reception of enamel. In no instance have the side loops, so common in bronze examples, been found on spear-heads of iron.

Arrow, or javelin-heads—generally differing from the spears, in size only—have been found in our principal crannogs; but no trace of a bow has, as far as I know, been recognized amongst the numerous relics formed of wood which usually accompany the metallic remains.

Axe-heads of a wedgelike form also occur; these were probably used in felling or splitting timber. A few present a form like the letter T.

Crannog Shields.—There can be little doubt, indeed, that our crannog dwellers—such of them at least as were able to bear arms—were in the possession of shields, some of which were formed of brass.

Not far from Lough Gur, a crannoged sheet of water in the county of Limerick—where, during drainage operations some forty years ago, a large number of bronze arms and implements were discovered—a very fine shield composed of bronze was accidentally brought to light. It is circular in plan (the diameter being 28 inches), and slightly convex; the centre rising about $1\frac{1}{4}$ inches above the rim; and the *umbo*, which is 6 inches wide at the base, rising in conical form $1\frac{3}{4}$ inches above the shield. " The hollow of the *umbo* in-

Bronze Shield from Lough Gur.

ternally is crossed by a stout handle, firmly riveted to the shield, of sheet bronze bent into a round. The metal of the shield is formed at the edge into a round hollow rim by being most skilfully turned inwards into a roll $\frac{1}{4}$ inch wide; between it and the *umbo* are six beaten-up circular ribs, and six rows of small studs. In the circle next the rim there are seventy-three studs, and in that next the *umbo* twenty-two. The

bronze, which is of a fine golden colour, is about the
thickness of a worn shilling next the rim, and of a six-
pence near the centre."

In our crannogs many pieces of hammered sheet
iron, which appear to have belonged to shields, have
from time to time been found. It is probable, however, that shields were, as a rule, formed of wood
covered with a piece of the hide of an animal such as
the deer or *bos longifrons.*

Crannog Boats.—Boats, or canoes fashioned out
of a single piece of timber, have been very frequently

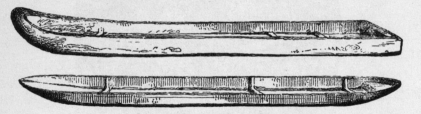

Crannog Boats.

discovered in nearly all our crannog-bearing inland
waters. Some examples are so small as to have been
capable of accommodating but one moderately-grown
person at a time; others are of surprising length and
beam, one from Lough Owel, preserved in the Collection of the Royal Irish Academy, measuring at
present 42 feet in length. It was originally probably
3 feet longer, by from 4 to 5 feet in width. A considerable number of these "dug-outs," as craft of the
kind are sometimes styled, are furnished at their extremities with handle-like projections by which they

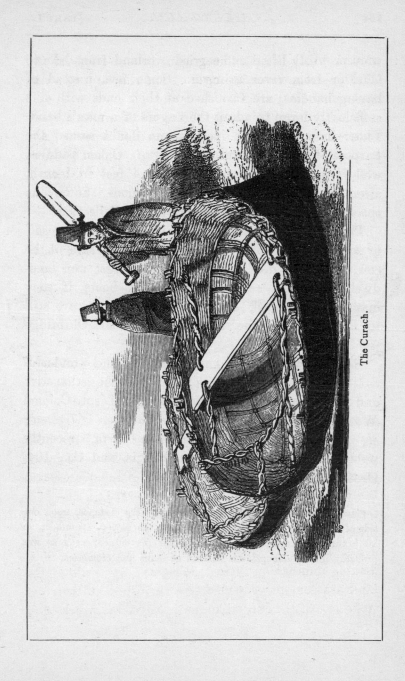

The Curach.

were probably lifted and carried overland from lake to
lake, or from river to river. Some few, instead of
having handles, are furnished at their ends with slits
sufficiently large to admit the fingers of a man's hand.
These indentations or incisions no doubt served the
purpose of the projections referred to. Oaken paddles,
well formed, and measuring about 4 feet in length,
often occur in connexion with the canoes. Some fine
specimens may be seen in the Academy Collection.

There is every reason to believe that the "*curach*"
or cot formed of basket-work, covered with skin of the
cow, horse, or deer, was in use amongst our lake-
dwellers. It is a curious fact that boats, if they
may be so termed, of this primitive class are still
to be found on the river Boyne, near Oldbridge
(see p. 263).*

Readers who would know more of the wonderful
contents of our crannogs are referred to the exhaustive
and highly-instructive compilation, by Lieut.-Colonel
Wood-Martin, entitled " *The Lake Dwellings of Ireland ;
or, Ancient Lacustrine Habitations of Erin,*" recently
published by Messrs. Hodges, Figgis, and Co., 104,
Grafton-street, Dublin.

---

* Ireland presents some curious contrasts. For instance, upon one
side of the bridge of Drogheda may be seen the modern steamboat, in
all luxurious completeness ; on the other the curach, such as was
probably in use amongst the builders of carns and cromleacs.

CHAPTER III.

MISCELLANEOUS FINDS—ECCLESIASTICAL FUR-NITURE, ETC., ETC.

WEAPONS AND IMPLEMENTS COMPOSED OF FLINT OR STONE—TORQUES AND GOLDEN ORNAMENTS—SWORDS, SPEAR-HEADS, CELTS, ETC., OF BRONZE— SEPULCHRAL URNS—QUADRANGULAR BELLS, RELIQUARIES, AND SHRINES—CROOKS AND CROZIERS—THE CROSS OF CONG—THE ARDAGH CHALICE—ORNAMENTED CASES FOR SACRED WRITINGS—WEAPONS OF IRON AND STEEL.

EGARDING the vast number of antiquities discovered from year to year (I might almost write, daily) in the bogs, beds of rivers, and newly-ploughed lands of Ireland, it is much to be regretted that the feeling which now very generally leads to the preservation of these evidences of ancient Irish skill in many of the arts, should have slept so long. Within comparatively recent times, if anyone were to inquire of a country watchmaker of a few years' standing, whether he had ever been offered for sale any antique ornaments of gold or silver, in ninety-nine cases out of a hundred his answer would be: "Yes, many; but, as there was no one to purchase them, I melted them down." If questioned as to their form and character, he would describe rings, fibulæ, bracelets, perhaps torcs, &c., generally adding that he regretted their destruction, as they were curiously engraved.

Bronze weapons, and articles of domestic use, suffered a similar fate in the foundries. Weapons, of stone or iron, being of no intrinsic value, were completely disregarded ; indeed, it is within the author's memory that any antiques of the latter were supposed to remain. At length a few private individuals of known learning and taste began to form collections. Forty or fifty years ago, antiques in Ireland were much more easily obtained than at present, and their success was very considerable. To form a museum then required neither the expenditure of much time nor money, and the example was soon followed by gentlemen in many parts of the country. Still, however, the destruction was only abated, and few of the collectors were possessed of sufficient knowledge to enable them to discriminate between objects of real national interest and such as would now be considered unimportant. The "Dublin Penny Journal," a weekly issue, in which numerous woodcuts, accompanied with letter-press descriptions of objects of Irish antiquarian interest, were for the first time presented to the public, did much to dispel this ignorance. Other publications followed, new collectors appeared, a general desire for information on the subject of our antiquities arose, and it is to be hoped that for many years back there have occurred few instances of the wanton destruction of any remarkable relic of the stone or metallurgic culture of ancient Ireland.

Amongst the illustrated publications referred to as having done good service to the cause of Irish archæology, Petrie's great work on the Round Towers and early Ecclesiastical Architecture of Ireland, in its particular province, has not been equalled. The quarterly "Journal of the Royal Historical and Archæological Association of Ireland," now the Royal Society of Antiquaries of Ireland, established over forty years ago and still flourishing, may be considered as having taken the highest place as a popular instructor in Irish antiquarian subjects. The "Catalogue of Irish Antiquities," preserved in the Museum of the Royal Irish Academy, and other works, most notably "The Boyne and Blackwater," and "Lough Corrib," from the pen of the late Sir William Wilde ; as also many admirably illustrated Papers by other members of the Academy, which from time to time appeared in the *Transactions* and *Proceedings* of that learned body, no doubt largely excited public interest in our ancient remains. Nor should the labours of the artists and writers who contributed to the pages of the "Ulster Journal of Archæology" be forgotten.

An attempt to describe, in a volume like this, any considerable number of the objects of antiquarian interest deposited in our public museums, or in the cabinets of private individuals, would prove utterly abortive ; but a glance at some of the most remarkable preserved in the collection of the Royal Irish Academy, now deposited in the Museum of Science and Art,

Kildare-street, cannot fail to interest many of my readers.

A history of that great institution, from the pen of Valentine Ball, M.R.I.A., its accomplished Director, is now in the press, and will ere long be published. The museum was originally founded, more than 150 years ago, by the Royal Dublin Society. The present system of administration by the Department of Science and Art only dates from the year 1877. The museum is by no means exclusively antiquarian in character; indeed, there is scarcely an intellectual taste that may not be within these noble halls abundantly gratified. It is the intention of the authorities to prepare for each department a carefully-compiled guide, or handbook, the cost of which, to the public, will not exceed a few pence. As the splendid collection of Irish antiquities belonging to the Royal Irish Academy has only lately been here deposited, some time, as the Director in his " General Guide " to the place intimates, " must necessarily elapse before it is in a condition to be described as arranged in its new habitation."

Weapons and Implements composed of Flint or Stone.—Antiquaries of late years have generally agreed to divide the objects formed of flint or stone, found in the British Islands, and indeed in other European countries, into two great classes—an earlier and a later. The former is supposed to comprise arms and implements of an epoch usually styled the " Palæolithic," when, as stated by Sir John Lubbock, " man shared the possession of Europe with the mammoth, the cave-bear, the woolly-haired rhinoceros, and other extinct animals. To the later, or "Neolithic" period, have been assigned all weapons or instruments composed of flint or stone, more or less polished, and often exhibiting elegance of design, and an elaborate degree of finish.

Our cabinets are far from rich in the possession of so-called " Palæolithic " remains, but some highly characteristic specimens may be seen in the collection of cave "finds" preserved in the National Museum, Kildare-street. Others occur in the Museum of the Royal Irish Academy.

Worked flints which had served the purposes of knives, scrapers, skinners, arrow, jave-lin, or spear-heads, chisels, borers, axe-heads, &c., &c., have been found in enor-

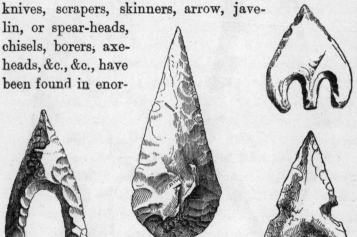

Arrow-heads formed of Flint. Drawn full size.

mous quantities in Ireland, and particularly in Ulster, where, in Antrim especially, the material is so

abundant.   They may be counted in hundreds in
our public and private museums; and though within

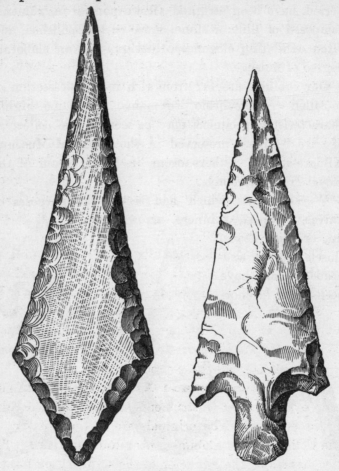

Spear or Javelin-heads of Flint.   Drawn full size.

the last twenty or thirty years they have been exported
to England, and to the continents of Europe and

America, in almost incredible numbers, they are still, in certain districts of the North, the subject of daily traffic.   It will scarcely be believed that not very long ago worked flints, comprising examples of almost every class, some exquisitely fashioned, used to be sold by their finders along the coasts of Antrim and Down, by the quart, for about the sum of one shilling !

It should be observed that, as the spirit of collecting increased, prices for these relics of a long past, but mysterious, period advanced in due proportion ; so much so as to induce certain native " Flint Jacks " to produce counterfeits, which were, and are, eagerly purchased by unsuspecting strangers, of which body, wonderful to say, American tourists are, it would appear, the most gullible.

The foregoing full-sized illustrations will afford an excellent idea of typical spear or javelin heads of flint, as found in Ireland.   They were drawn by myself for the " Catalogue of Irish Antiquities," compiled for the Academy by the late Sir William Wilde.   By the kindness of the Council of that body I am enabled here to reproduce them.

Stone Hammers and Axe-Heads.—Four cuts annexed represent instruments of the kind notified in the heading.   The originals are in the Museum of the College of St. Columba, near Rathfarnham.   The two figures on the left refer to the ordinary perforated stone hammer, or pick, which is often found in connexion with worked flints, in the manufacture of which it is assumed by many archæologists they were used.

Beautifully designed and highly polished axe-heads of a larger kind, and formed of stone apparently selected for its hardness, have not unfrequently been found in

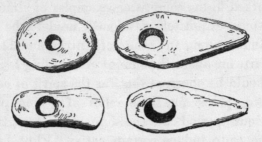

Ordinary Stone Hammers and Axe-heads.

the British Islands. These are usually considered to have been battle-axes, of a comparatively late, but still pagan period. In the collection of the Academy

No. 1.   No. 2.
BATTLE-AXES OF STONE.

No. 1.—Eight inches and three-quarters in length. Material, serpentine.

No. 2.—Nine inches and three-eights in length. Material, fine-grained hornblendic syenite.

are a number of truly fine examples, two of which are here figured. The larger is composed of fine-grained hornblendic syenite. With us they usually occur in Ulster; and are, for the most part, formed of varieties of basalt, a material very common in the counties of

Antrim and Down.   Students in archæology should see
a highly elaborate implement of this kind preserved in
the Petrie collection, Royal Irish Academy, and also
another one belonging to the
Museum of the Science and
Art Department.

By far the most common
of the stone remains found
in Ireland are hatchet-shaped
implements commonly called
celts.   Of these a very great
number occur in the Aca-
demy's museum.   They are of
sizes varying from 22 inches
to 1¾ inches in length.   The
smaller specimens were doubtlessly set in the end of a stick,
and used as chisels in the
manufacture of wooden vessels
or other light work.   Others,
there is reason to believe, were
simply held in the hand, and
served the double purpose of
cutting instruments and hammers.   By the edge, more or
less sharp, animal food or in-

Axe-head of Stone.

teguments might be carved, or at least roughly divided,
while by aid of the opposite end, which is almost invariably blunt or flat, marrow-bearing bones might be
smashed.

In all probability, however, the great majority had
been the heads of axes used for every-day purposes,
or as weapons of war.   They are most frequently
discovered in ancient river fords, the passage of
which had, no doubt, been frequently contested.   In
some very rare instances the stone has been found
still attached to an original handle of wood.   It
is most likely that some remains of this class were

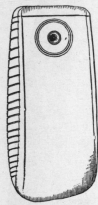

used as projectiles.   We read of a
missive weapon called the *Lia Lamha
Laich*, i. e. a " champion's handstone,"
which was carried ready for use in
the hollow of the shield.   It is described by early writers in a manner
which shows that it was attached to a
line of some kind, and was recoverable
after each cast.   O'Curry suggests that
missiles of this kind were simply our
stone celts.   There can be little doubt
of the correctness of his opinion.   In
the collection of the Academy are

Supposed Champion
Stone for Casting.

three stones of that description, which at their narrow
end exhibit perforations well adapted for the attach-
ment of a string or line.   The largest of these stones
is slightly over $3\frac{1}{2}$ inches in length.   Its sides are
crossed by arrays of scorings, admirably adapted for
the purpose of affording an unslipping grasp to a
champion desirous of hurling the stone with force.
Around the aperture are two engraved circles.   The
other perforated celts are sharp and well formed, but

plain.   Each would constitute a formidable missile when cast by a trained hand.

Torques, and Golden Ornaments, &c.—There is abundant evidence, historical and other, that even in the most remote days of which Erin possesses any record, her people were in the habit of manufacturing ornaments and articles of luxury or necessity, the material of which was gold.

The "Annals of the Four Masters," at A.M. 3656, state " it was by Tighernmas " (king of Ireland) " that gold was first smelted in Ireland in Foithre-Airthir-Liffe.   (It was) Uchadan, an artificer of the Fera-Cualann, smelted it.   It was by him that goblets and brooches were first covered with gold and silver in Ireland."   A very similar entry occurs in the " Annals of Clonmacnoise."   The district referred to is included in the county of Wicklow, and part of that of Dublin.   It is a very remarkable fact that even to this day gold is found in several of the mountain streams of Wicklow.   In the Museum of the Science and Art Department, Kildare-street, may be seen the model of a Wicklow nugget which weighed 22 ounces.   One has been found of nine and another of eight ounces.   It has been computed that from about the commencement of the present century the jewellers of Dublin have paid annually an average sum of £2000 for nuggets from Wicklow streams, secretly sold to them by the finders.   Sir William Wilde, who had personally visited every considerable collection of antiquities in Europe, has stated that

Ireland possesses a greater number of golden antiques
than may be seen in all the British and Continental
Museums taken together. He thus classifies the
golden articles preserved in the Museum of the Royal
Irish Academy :—" Diadems, tiaras, lunulæ, hair-
plates, and ear-rings; those used for the neck, as,
for example, gorgets, small torques, flattened beads,
globular balls, and necklaces; for the limbs, as armillæ,
bracelets, finger-rings ; and for the chest and waist in
the form of large torques, besides several minor trinkets
and miscellaneous articles, such as bullæ, small circular boxes, penannular-shaped articles supposed to
represent money, and some other objects of undeter-
mined use."

Notwithstanding the immense number of golden
treasures found in Ireland, and preserved in one
museum or another, antiquaries cannot but deplore
the loss and destruction of many hundreds of examples.
For instance, in 1860, a letter appeared in the " Athe-
næum " from Mr. Clibborn the then Curator of the
Museum of the Royal Irish Academy, stating "that a
considerable gold find had been made near Athlone to the
value of £27,000, which had been entirely lost to the antiquarian world." Again, in 1854, during the construction
of the Limerick and Ennis Railway, certain labourers
found under a rude carn an untold treasure of the
precious metal. So great was this find that four days
after the discovery four men departed to America
with about £6,000 each. Large numbers of the
objects were immediately melted down in Limerick

and neighbouring towns ; a few only seem to have
been saved from oblivion.

The subject of the annexed illustration is a group of
four torques of the usual kind. The two outer

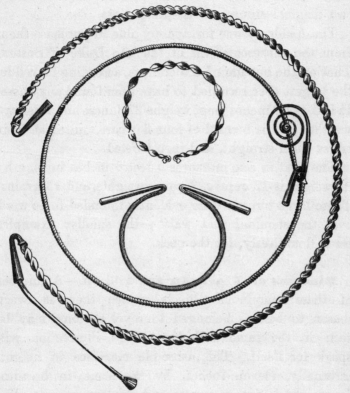

Golden Torques, Museum of the Royal Irish Academy.

examples were dug out of a bank of earth on the Hill
of Tara. This was in 1810, a time when scarcely any-

thing was known about our antiquities, and the torques
were hawked about the streets of Navan for sale as
old brass, but nobody would purchase them. They
were found in the immediate vicinity of the monuments identified by Petrie as Mael Bloc and Bluicni,
two magical stones of the pillar class.

The Academy was fortunately able to purchase them
from the representatives of the late Duke of Sussex.
That on the outside of the circle is, according to Wilde,
the largest ever recorded to have been found anywhere.
It is 5 feet 7 inches long, weighs 27 ounces and 7 pennyweights, and is formed of four flat bars, united at their
edges when straight, and then twisted.

The next in size measures 5 feet 6 inches in length;
its weight is 12 ounces, 7 pennyweights, and 13 grains.
These large torques were evidently intended to be worn
over the shoulder and waist; the smaller examples
were, doubtlessly, for the neck.

Diadems or Tiaras in Irish ᵐᵢⁿ'ᵒ.—A number
of these sumptuous objects, which there is every
reason to believe belonged to royal persons, may be
seen in the same collection. The illustration will
speak for itself. This example measures in height,
internally, eleven inches, by the same in breadth.
Its weight is sixteen ounces and thirteen grains. The
minʋ is supposed to have been worn over the forehead
and sides of the face, the discs covering the ears.
Some antiquaries believe that it was a Celtic form of

crown. Attention should be paid to the wonderful display of minor articles of gold, such as rings, fibulæ, &c., &c., exhibited.

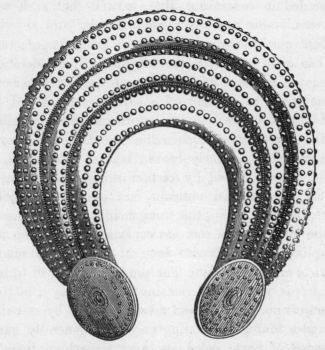

Mind, or Diadem, of Gold, Museum of the Royal Irish Academy.

Swords, Spearheads, Celts, &c., &c., of Bronze. —Petrie used to relate that on the occasion of the visit of Mr. Dodwell to Dublin, that that keen observer, on seeing a collection of our ancient swords and other weapons formed of bronze, exclaimed: "Where did you get those wonderful Greek swords and spears? Finer specimens of the antique bronze it would be

impossible to find." "Petrie assured him that they
were not found in Greece, but in Ireland. Yet he
used to say that he was by no means sure of having
succeeded in convincing Mr. Dodwell that such was
the case."—See Stokes's "Life of Petrie."

That our bronze weapons are of home manufacture
no one who has given the subject any consideration
can for a moment doubt. Though bearing a general
resemblance to remains of a similar class found in
Britain and on the European continent, the nationality
of the majority of such relics found in the bogs,
beds of rivers, or newly broken land of this island, is
sufficiently indicated by certain minute peculiarities
which, to a skilled observer, are almost invariably
perceptible. Besides, the stone moulds in which many
of the objects were cast are constantly turned up by
the plough, or otherwise brought to light in many
districts of the country. The precise manner in which
the swords were hafted remained until lately a matter
of conjecture. It has been shown, however, by existing
examples that the mounting may very generally have
consisted of bone; wood also may have been largely
used. It is curious to observe that, while in the
northern and other districts of the Continent of
Europe bronze swords are commonly found with
handles of the same metal, we cannot point to a
single Irish specimen so furnished. True it is that
rapiers and dagger knives of bronze, the blades and
handles of which are of the same material, occasionally
with us occur. In the accompanying illustration are

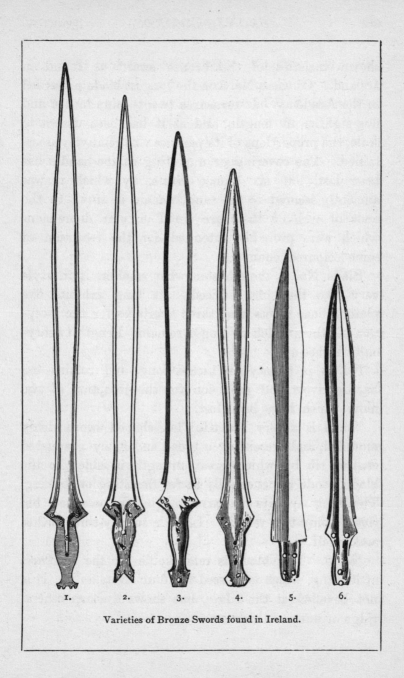

Varieties of Bronze Swords found in Ireland.

shown varieties of the bronze sword as found in Ireland. Of these No. 1 is the longest blade preserved in the Academy. It measures twenty-nine inches and five-eighths in length, and as it has been drawn to scale, the proportions of its parts can be relatively ascertained. The covering or mounting of the handle has been lost, but six bronze rivets, by which it was anciently secured to the tang, remain *in situ*. In the ends of each of these are small circular depressions which were probably intended for the reception of some coloured enamel.

Blade No. 2, though somewhat smaller, is in style very like that just noticed. Its tang exhibits five plain bronze rivets, and three apertures for the reception of others which no longer remain. Length twenty-eight inches and a-half.

No. 3 is twenty-six inches long, and retains ten handle rivets and provision for the reception of two more which have been lost.

No. 4 is a very beautiful leaf-shaped sword richly moulded, and presenting a broad and finely graduated central rib by which great strength is added to the blade, rendering it equally fit for thrusting or striking. The tang appears to have originally possessed ten rivets; only two remain. Length twenty-three inches and a-half.

No. 5. This blade is remarkable for the shortness of its tang, which is pierced for four rivets only. It is not bevelled at the edges, but shows a sharp central ridge of unusual thickness.

The rapiers partake very much of the character of the swords, and are unquestionably from the same school of manufacture. Except in the circumstance of being usually very long and narrow in the blade, they, as a rule, differ in little from the swords and daggers with which they are sometimes found. Several moulds of stone, which had been used for the purpose of casting this class of weapon, are recorded to have been discovered in Ireland. As has already been remarked, they were, like the daggers, occasionally furnished with handles of bronze. There is reason to believe that their mounting was usually formed of bone. But one example of an early bronze sword-sheath is known to have been found in Ireland. This is now in the collection of Robert Day, F.S.A., of Cork.

Dagger hafted with Bronze.

Spear and Javelin-heads of Bronze.—Amongst the antiquarian treasures preserved in the Museum of the Royal Irish Academy, are bronze spear-heads, many of which are remarkable for their elegance of form, and as presenting evidence of the wonderful skill of their fabricators in the art of metallurgy. Scores of examples at least equal in interest and beauty to the five here figured may be seen in the collection.

No. 1 is, with a single exception, the largest spear-head known to have been discovered in Ireland. It is 2 feet 6¾ inches in length; is composed of fine golden-coloured metal, run very light and thin; and is furnished near the socket, as is

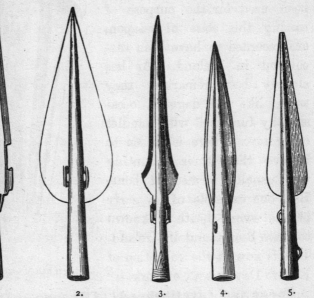

1.   2.   3.   4.   5.

Varieties of Spear-heads of Bronze.

usual in such remains, with two loops which were probably intended for the reception of a line or string, by which after a cast, successful or otherwise, the weapon could be recovered.

No. 2, which measures 13½ inches in length, is composed, like No. 1, of bright golden-coloured bronze. It is remarkable for the breadth of its blade, and for the position of its loops as shown in the illustration.

No. 3 presents a very unusual form, being concave on its curved sides. Here, as usual, we find loops upon the socket; they, however, present a somewhat rare feature, being connected with the base of the blade by narrow lateral fillets. The socket, it will be observed, is at its end richly engraved with lines and chevrons like those which are found in great variety upon many of our sepulchral urns. Length, 15 inches.

No. 4.—This is an excellent example of the leaf-shaped spear-head so well known to collectors of Irish antiquities. Here we find no side loops, but the socket is pierced for the reception of a rivet, which was probably of wood, by which the head was secured to the shaft or handle. It may be observed that the sockets of this class of remains are almost invariably of abnormal diameter, and that the metal of the head is usually of a duller colour, and apparently more coppery, if I may use the term, than that of ordinary antique bronze. Size, 13½ inches.

In No. 5 we have a very curious specimen, composed of true bronze. Its great peculiarity is in the position of the side loops—one appearing near the end of the socket, while the other is considerably above it, and nearly immediately under the side of the blade. The

loops, too, are of unusual character, being almost semicircular in form, while features of their kind are, as a
general rule, shaped either as a lozenge or an oblong
rectangle. The socket is quite plain. Length, 13⅞
inches.

Ornamented Spears.—The spear-head indicated
by fig. 1 in the accompanying illustration measures
7½ inches in length. It is a charming
example in every respect, and when first

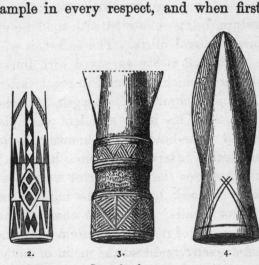

Ornaments on Spear-heads.

lifted from the bed of the Shannon was as bright as
gold. It has no patina, and is now of a dull yellow
colour. I shall not here essay to describe the ornamentation. Nos. 1 and 2 will do that better than
words. No. 2 is drawn upon a larger scale than
that adopted in the general view of the spear-head,
in order to bring out the decorative designs with

clearness. The work is wonderfully similar to some
that appears on golden lunettes and other relics of
presumably prehistoric days treasured in the Academy
collection. No. 3 illustrates the socket of a spear-head
boldly and richly decorated in the same style of art.
No. 4 is a full-sized engraving of the smallest bronze
spear, or javelin-head, preserved in the collection.
Like No. 4 of the group of spear-heads already given,
it is composed of dark-coloured bronze, and exhibits,
for the size of the object, a most disproportionate
diameter in the socket.

Celts of Bronze, &c.—The most common weapon or weapon-tool, in use amongst the inhabitants of
Ireland during a remote, but undefined period, was an
instrument of which several varieties are known, commonly called a celt. Its material, except in some
very rare instances, is bronze; and it appears to have
been used contemporaneously with swords and spear-
heads, of which examples have just been given.

The ordinary bronze celt is rarely more than seven
inches in length, and several have been preserved
which scarcely measure an inch and a-half. There
are two kinds: the more common is flat and wedge-
shaped, and, like its stone namesake, appears to have
been fixed by the smaller end into a wooden handle;
the other is hollow, and furnished by a small ear or
loop, through which it has been supposed a string
securing it to the handle anciently passed. From
remains still extant it is evident that these implements
were, at times at least, mounted on a curved shaft or

handle of wood, and used as axes or choppers : but
there is no reason to assume that the handle was not
generally a straight piece of worked wood, ash, or oak,
or growth of some other tough description, and the
implement used as we do a chisel.   Some of these
so-called "socketed celts" are so diminutive that they

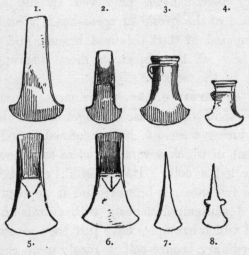

Celts, Paalstaves, and Implements of Bronze.

could not have served for chopping of any kind. Fixed
at the end of a wooden handle, they, no doubt, might
well answer the purpose of chisels. No. 1 in the
illustration figures the ordinary plain flat celt which
varies in dimensions from a couple of inches or so to
nearly a foot. The larger and medium-sized examples
may have been used, when set in a proper handle, as
battle-axes.

    Nos. 3 and 4 show the form of the socketed celt, as

most commonly discovered in Ireland. Nos. 7 and 8
were certainly chisels. Though often found with the
socketed celts, objects of this kind form a different
class. Of their handles no trace has hitherto been
found, or, at least, recorded.

Socketed Celts from the Academy Collection.

Many of the socketed celts preserved in the Academy
collection are richly ornamented, and not a few of them
are highly interesting on account of their peculiarity
of form. It would seem that instruments of this kind
are found in every country of Europe, more especially
in the north and west, and that, as a general rule,
each district exhibits its own particular type. For

instance, No. 9 is of a form very unusual in Ireland,
in which country, however, it was certainly discovered.
It measures 5⅜ inches in length. Possibly it is an
ancient importation from Britain. No. 10 is, with us,
of very rare type; length, 4½ inches. Nos. 11 and 12
are highly decorated, as shown in the illustration; the
former is 4½ inches long; the latter is given half its
real size. Nos. 13 and 14 are each, as nearly as
possible, 4 inches in length, and are highly characteristic of the plainer class of Irish socketed celt.

Intermediate between the implements just noticed
and the " paalstave," an in-
strument   presently   to   be
referred to, is a kind of celt
which   seems   to   have   answered all the purposes for
which the others were intended.   Usually,   near   its
centre, or rather closer to the
blunt end, is a slight rise
in the metal, or a shallow

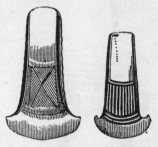

Decorated Flat Celts, partaking
of the Paalstave Class.

transverse ridge, evidently intended as a stop to the
handle when forced downwards. Two tastefully ornamented examples are here represented, each about one-
third the real size. It will be noticed that the designs
which in their carving they exhibit are exactly similar
to the work often seen upon cinerary urns, as well as
upon lunettes, &c., &c., of gold.

Closely akin to the celts, and often found along
with them, is the implement already alluded to,

which, for want of a better name, is usually styled
a paalstave.

Of their general appearance the following illustration
will convey a sufficiently accurate idea. The handle
was inserted between the flanges which
project at the sides, and
was, doubtlessly, further se-

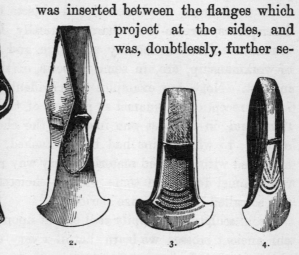

Paalstaves of Bronze.

cured by a ligature of some kind coiled round the
butt-end of the implement. Paalstaves are rarely
looped at their sides. But two specimens, as far as
I am aware, have been found in Ireland, which
exhibit a double feature of that kind, as in No. 1.
The loop is almost invariably single. No. 2 is furnished on each side by a projecting knob, by which,
no doubt, the lashing was anciently secured from
slipping. Its flanges are bold and projecting; and,
as usual, are slightly curved inwards, so as in a
manner to grasp the handle. Nos. 3 and 4 are richly

engraved in archaic style, and in their day must have been considered very beautiful.

Bridle-bits, &c.—Amongst the rarer remains of a period when bronze was very largely used in the production of arms, implements, and objects of various descriptions, bridle-bits, characteristically Irish, and remarkable for their beauty of design and excellence of workmanship, are, in some respects, of the highest interest. Not a few examples were evidently intended for the reception of enamel as portion of their decoration; and, in at least one instance, the check-pieces, or rings to which reins had been attached, are richly embossed with coloured material, every way resembling the enamel found on some of our choicest relics of the so-called "late bronze period."

From sculptures, happily still extant upon several of our ancient crosses, we learn that at a very early time chariots were in use amongst, as may be presumed, some of the higher ranks—ecclesiastical and other—of the people of Ireland. The vehicles are represented as furnished with large-sized, spoked wheels, and drawn by pairs of high-stepping, evidently mettlesome, steeds. The body of the machine is quite elegant in design, and we have records that it was at times artistically embellished with *findruine*, a white metal more precious amongst the ancient Irish than silver. Horse trappings composed of bronze richly gilt, and displaying admirable examples of the *Opus Hibernicum*, are not unusual in our museums. At Tara was a space known as the " Slope of the Chariots," where we may suppose

races were held. From that historic eminence roads
radiated north, south, and west. These highways,
planned about the first century A. D., were constructed,
as may be judged from traces of them which still
remain, in the Roman fashion. See Wilde's "Boyne
and Blackwater."

The three bronze bridle-bits here figured may be
seen in the collection of the Academy. Nos. 1 and 2

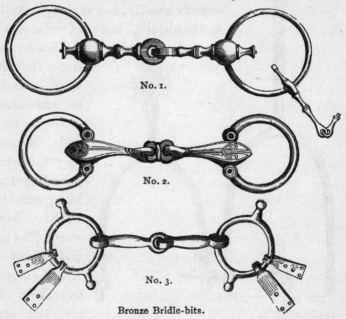

No. 1.

No. 2.

No. 3.

Bronze Bridle-bits.

are peculiarly Celtic in style, and if discovered in Britain
would be considered as older than the period of Roman
occupation in that country. No. 3, which was found
near Navan, Co. Meath, accompanied with gilt bronze
trappings, and the skull and other remains of a horse

is most likely of a later period than the others. Almost immediately with it were a dozen or so human skeletons, and traces of cremation. In general form and in its details this bit closely resembles some specimens formed of iron which were dug out from the crannogs of Lagore and Ardakillen.*

In immediate proximity to bronze-bits of the earlier kind, spur-shaped objects usually, but vaguely described as "headstalls," have not unfrequently been discovered. There is some evidence that they were attached to the check-pieces, or rings, and for some as yet unascertained purpose hung with their knobs downward. The central figure in No. 1 is given to show the style of ornamentation that appears upon the external sides of the terminal loops. The lines,

No. 1.   No. 2.

Trappings of Bronze, called "Headstalls," found with Bronze Bridle-bits.

* See Col. Wood-Martin's "Irish Lake Dwellings." Dublin. 1886.

which are deeply cut, were probably enamelled. Altogether the work seems to point to a period when our artists in bronze knew well how to produce ornamented designs remarkable for chasteness, and, it may even be said, Etruscan elegance. In No. 2 the crosslike figures are very curious and remarkable, but they need not be supposed to bear any reference to Christian symbolism.

Yokes, formed of wood, by which steeds, oxen, or other animals of draught were coupled, have often been found in our peat bogs. Some examples exhibit much taste in their style of decoration. See a specimen preserved in the Academy Collection.

Cauldrons.—So long ago as the mythic days of the Tuatha de Danaans, cauldrons, in Irish coɪɲe, formed

Bronze Cauldron, Academy Collection.

of thin plates of beaten bronze, curiously riveted together, appear to have been common in this country. They are usually of very graceful form, and were furnished with two rings, or handles, placed opposite

to each other, at or near the rim of the vessel. Most
of the known specimens must have been long in use, as
they are generally more or less patched and mended in
places where the metal had given way. The added
pieces are of the same material as the body of the
utensil, and are kept in position by rivets, never by
soldering. They were probably used for cooking purposes, but one vessel of this class was discovered nearly
full of celts, paalstaves, daggers, crotals, and other
objects of bronze.

Cauldrons are constantly mentioned in our venerable
manuscripts. In the " Book of Rights," as quoted by
Mr. George Langtry in the pages of the "Journal" of the
Royal Irish Society of Antiquaries of Ireland, vol. III.,
Fourth Series, p. 22, the following passages occur :—

> " A cauldron is given to the King of Cashel
> By the King of Teamhair, the mighty chief,
> To be presented in due form,
> And to be brought to Teamhair Luachra."

And again :—

> " Entitled is the King of Laithne to this,
> To a steed and to two score of cows,
> For his rising out is not less,
> Neither is his cauldron or his vat."

Cauldrons formed of iron, exactly similar in shape
and style of workmanship to those of bronze, have
very recently been found in Ireland. Canon Grainger's
collection, now in Belfast, contains two highly valuable
examples from the crannog of Lisnacroghera, Co.

Antrim.   A third, from Lough Erne, was, about two
years ago, presented to the Royal Irish Academy by
Seaton Milligan, Esq.

War Trumpets of Bronze.—Bronze trumpets,
apparently coeval with the beautiful weapons recently
noticed, have frequently been found in various parts of
the country. In the group here represented the largest

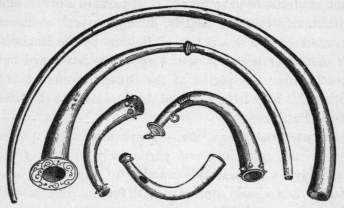

Bronze Trumpets, Academy Collection.

measures 8 ft. 5 in. in length. As the others are drawn
to the same scale their respective dimensions can be easily
ascertained. When not in use they were probably slung
from the shoulder, some of the instruments exhibiting
loops to which straps could be attached. They were
blown from an aperture in the side ; and with little
difficulty some of them may still be used so as to emit
a sound loud enough to warn a friend or terrify an
enemy. Curiously enough, horns almost exactly similar
in form to our Celtic trumpets are in use amongst some

of the wilder African tribes. They, however, are made
of horn or ivory, never of metal. As may be seen in
the woodcut, one of the Academy specimens exhibits at
its broader termination an exquisite scroll, wrought in
the style usually termed "late Celtic." Decoration of
this chaste description is supposed, by Mr. Franks of
the British Museum, perhaps the highest authority on
such subjects, to have prevailed in parts of Europe, and
particularly in these islands, during several centuries
previous to the occupation of Britain by the Romans.
In the sister island it would appear to have died out
shortly after the period of the invasion referred to ;
with us, it may have lingered down almost to the time
of St. Patrick.

Sepulchral Urns, &c.—There are in our public
and private museums, and particularly in that of the
Academy, a considerable number of sepulchral urns
and earthen vessels connected with funeral rites, several
of which may challenge comparison with any hitherto
discovered in Great Britain.

Vessels of this description have of late been classified
under three headings, viz. :—Urns proper, which were
intended for the reception of calcined human bones;
food vessels, usually found with the former ; and
"Incense Cups," so called for want of a more definite
name.

The urns are generally somewhat slender in figure,
and are usually decorated with chevron, lozenge, or
other archaic designs impressed into the clay. A good
many of the richer description present mouldings,

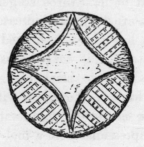

Scale of Inches.

W.F.Wakeman.
1888.

**Side and Bottom of a Cinerary Urn from a Tomb in Co. Carlow,
discovered by Colonel Vigors.**

bosses, &c., in relief. It is most difficult to form an exact opinion as to the manner in which the majority of our more highly decorated and larger urns were manufactured. They generally present an outer surface, some eighth or so of an inch in depth, composed apparently of well-kneaded compost of yellow or buff-coloured clay, which exhibits but few or no traces of the action of fire. Underneath this envelope is a black highly-fused mass of coarser composition, which forms what may be called the strength of the vessel. It is a fact—strange but true—that the majority of our cinerary vases exhibit upon the interior indications of an intense action of fire, while in many examples the outer surface would seem to be simply sun-baked. From a most careful examination of a considerable number of urns found in Irish tumuli or sandhills, it seems to me pretty certain that at least three stages in the process of their formation are distinctly indicated. Firstly, the vessel appears to have been fashioned of a somewhat coarse, gritty material ; it was then baked in a strong fire, and burnt almost to blackness. It would seem, upon cooling, to have been overlaid with a fine matter, generally buff or cream-coloured, sufficiently soft to readily receive impressions from a tool formed of wood, horn, bone, stone, or possibly of bronze or iron. Strips of light material, like that of the coating or veneer already referred to, were then laid on, just (to use a homely illustration), as a modern cook will embellish a pie-crust. The overlayings, while still soft, were then indented with patterns, and the work either dried in

the sun or presented to the influence of a moderate
degree of heat from a fire of wood or peat.

All our sepulchral urns were hand-made, and are
invariably unglazed. They have been found to contain portions of the bones of a human body, sometimes
of more than one, in a highly calcined state ; and

Sepulchral Urns from Co. Down.

there is reason to believe that occasionally some relics,
also burnt, most notably those of the dog, had been
inurned along with the remains of man. Arrow-
heads and knives of flint, pins of bone or bronze, glass
and stone beads, rings of jet, and in one case, at least, a
beautiful knife or dagger of bronze, have formed with
the bones portion of the contents of these vessels; charcoal and particles of half-consumed wood constituting

the remainder. Sometimes the urn is found placed
mouth downward, and, as at Drumnakilly, surmounting a cup-hollow ; but in general it stands on its
base, and is covered by a thin flat stone or slate. A
unique and very beautiful example, preserved in the
Academy collection, is furnished with a veritable lid.
Though generally presenting the appearance of a mortuary urn, this relic may have been a food vessel.

The vessel usually considered to have been a receptacle
for food intended for the use of a departed soul on its
way to *Tir-na-n'og,* or " Land of the Young," or fairies,

No. 1.—Supposed Food Vessel from Cist in the Phœnix Park, Dublin.

the Valhalla of pagan Erin, is somewhat globular in
form, and is well represented in cut No. 1, which
figures a specimen discovered in connexion with the
cromleac-like tomb in the Phœnix Park, already
described. This vessel, with some antiquities of the
same " find," may be seen in the Academy collection.
One other example (No. 2), remarkable for the elaborate character of its ornamentation, is from Ballymote,

Co. Sligo. This cut, drawn by myself, originally appeared in Colonel Wood-Martin's " Rude Stone Monuments of Ireland."

No. 2.—Supposed Food Vessel from Tomb near Ballymote, Co. Sligo.

The so-called "Incense Cups," found in Ireland, are, like their British prototypes, invariably of extremely small size. They are usually undecorated. The rims are sometimes pierced with four or more apertures, as if for suspension. Vessels of this kind are, with us, usually found enclosed in urns of the larger and richer class. The purpose for which they were intended has not been ascertained.

CHAPTER IV.

ECCLESIASTICAL REMAINS IN THE COLLECTION OF THE
ROYAL IRISH ACADEMY.

BELLS, CROZIERS, SHRINES, ETC., ETC.; AND SOME MISCELLANEOUS
ANTIQUITIES FOUND NEAR DUBLIN.

ORDER to afford the reader an insight to the character of the collection generally, it will be as well to pass at once to objects of the early Christian period, a class of antiquities in which the Academy is also rich. Among these the ancient quadrangular bells of iron or bronze are, perhaps, not the least interesting. Bells appear to have been used in Ireland as early as the time of St. Patrick. They are mentioned in the lives of most of the early saints, in the " Annals of the Four Masters," and in other ancient compositions. Cambrensis, in his " Welsh Itinerary," says that both the laity and clergy in Ireland, Scotland, and Wales, held in much veneration certain portable bells; that they were much more afraid of swearing falsely by them than by the Gospels, " because of some hidden and miraculous power with which they were gifted;

and by the vengeance of the saint, to whom they were particularly pleasing, their despisers and transgressors were severely punished." The bells so highly reverenced by the Irish during the middle ages had severally belonged to some one of the early founders of Christianity in this island, and had been preserved in the time of the saint in a monastery which he had originally founded, or elsewhere, in the custody of hereditary keepers.

In like manner the pastoral crooks and croziers which had belonged to the early fathers of the Irish Church, appear to have been regarded as holy. Notwithstanding the frequent pillage of church property by the Danes, and the unsparing destruction of "superstitious" relics during the comparatively late period, numerous examples, remarkable for the beauty of their decorations and the excellence of their workmanship, have been preserved to our own times. There is scarcely any variety in the form of the early crooks; they are simply curved like those used by shepherds; but they usually exhibit a profusion of ornament, consisting of elaborately interwoven bands, terminating generally in serpents' heads, or in some equally singular device. In several specimens settings formed of stones, or an artificial substance, variously coloured, occur, but this is supposed to indicate a comparatively recent date. A visitor to the Academy Collection may inspect several examples remarkable as well for their extreme beauty, as for the excellent state of preservation in which they remain.

The Cross of Cong.—The Cross of Cong, the gem
of the Academy Collection, not only from its historical
associations, but also as it affords most striking evidence
of the advancement which the Irish artificers had made

The Cross of Cong.

in several of the arts, and in general manufacturing
skill, previous to the arrival of the English. It was
made at Roscommon by native Irishmen, about the
year 1123, in the reign of Turlough O'Conor, father

of Roderick, the last monarch of Ireland, and contained what was supposed to be a piece of the true cross, as inscriptions in Irish and Latin in the Irish character, upon two of its sides, distinctly record.*

The ornaments generally consist of tracery and grotesque animals, fancifully combined, and similar in character to the decorations found upon crosses of stone of about the same period. A large crystal, through which a portion of the wood which the cross was formed to enshrine is visible, is set in the centre at the intersection. The Academy owes the possession of this unequalled monument of ancient Irish art to the liberality of the late Professor Mac Cullagh, by whom it was purchased for the sum of one hundred guineas and presented.

Among the more singular relics in the collection, a chalice of stone is well worthy of observation. Though formed of so rude a material, there is nothing in its general form or in the character of its decorations to warrant a supposition that it belongs to a very early period. Few chalices of an age prior to the twelfth century remain in Ireland, and any of a later which have come under the observation of the writer are not very remarkable. A chalice of silver found in the ruins of Kilmallock Abbey was melted some years ago by a silversmith of Limerick into whose hands it had fallen. Cups of stone appear not to have been uncommon among the Irish. An ancient vessel of that

* See "Irish Grammar," by Dr. O'Donovan, page 234.

material, of a triangular form, remains, or very lately remained, by the side of a holy well in Columbkill's Glen, in the county of Clare; and another was found some years ago in the county of Meath, near the ruins of Ardmulchan Church.

The most remarkable object of the chalice class known to have been found in Ireland is the famous Ardagh Cup, or Chalice, which figures amongst the choicest examples of metal work preserved in the collection of the Academy. It has been fully described by the late Lord Dunraven (a Vice-President of the Academy) in the *Transactions* of that body. It, together with some silver brooches of exquisite workmanship, was discovered by a youth while digging potatoes in a rath situated not far from Ardagh, County Limerick. The material is silver, or, as thought by some experts, white bronze, and the vessel is richly encrusted with golden filigree and enamel of various colours. There are no fewer than 354 pieces, if we include 20 rivets, in the composition of this truly wonderful work. "The most remarkable feature is an inscription in peculiar square-formed letters giving the names of the Twelve Apostles—St. Paul being included. This runs round the cup under a gold band; but the outline being faint, the letters are not easily legible. The spaces between are stippled so as to form a shaded background."*

The Bell of Armagh.—Amongst the ecclesiastical bells preserved in the Academy Collection is one bear-

---

* See " Brief Handbook " for visitors to the collection.

ing the above title, and of surpassing interest, inasmuch
as there is every reason to believe that it had belonged
to St. Patrick himself. For many ages it was one of
the chief treasures preserved in Armagh, where it received the highest reverence, so much so that about the
close of the eleventh century it was enclosed in a magnificent and costly shrine, which happily still remains to
attract the wonder and admiration of all beholders.
The shrine bears an inscription, in the Irish character
and language, of which a translation by the late Rev.
Dr. Todd runs as follows:—"A prayer for Donnell
O'Lochlain, through whom this Bell (or Bell-shrine)
was made; and for Donnell, the successor of Patrick,
with whom it was made; and for Calahan O'Mulhollan,
the keeper of the Bell; and for Cudulig O'Inmainen,
with his sons, who covered (it)."

The Clog Beannaighthe.—A second bell from
Armagh is here shown. It bears the following in-
scription in Irish:—OROIT AR chumascach m̄
Ailello (Pray for Chumascach, son of Ailell). This
was a bell which originally belonged to the church of
Armagh. The death of the individual mentioned in
the inscription is recorded in the "Annals of the Four
Masters" as occurring in A.D. 909.

The copies of the Gospels and other sacred writings
which had been used by the early saints of Ireland
were generally preserved by their successors, enclosed
in cases formed of yew or some wood equally durable.
Many of those cases were subsequently enshrined or
enclosed in boxes of silver, or of bronze richly plated

with silver and occasionally gilt; and in several instances a third case appears to have been added. Sir William Betham, in his "Irish Antiquarian Researches," describes several of those evidences of early Irish piety still extant and remaining in a high state of preservation. They are the Caah or Cathac, the Meeshac, and the Leabhar Dhimma.

The Clog Beannaighthe.

The Caah, which has been deposited in the Museum of the Academy, is a box about nine inches and a-half in length, eight in breadth, and two in thickness, formed of brass plates riveted one to the other and ornamented with gems and chasings in gold and silver. It contains as usual a rude wooden box " enclosing a

MS. on vellum, a copy of the ancient Vulgate translation of the Psalms in Latin consisting of fifty-eight
membranes." This MS. there is every reason to believe
was written by the hand of St. Columba, or Columkille,
the Apostle of the northern Picts, and founder of an
almost incredible number of monasteries in Ireland, his
native country. A glance at the decoration displayed
upon the top of the box will convince the critical
antiquary of the comparatively late date of this portion
of the relic. The top is ornamented with a silver
plate richly gilt, and divided into three compartments
by clustered columns supporting arches. The central
space is somewhat larger than the others, and contains
the figure of an ecclesiastic, probably St. Columba, who
is represented in a sitting posture giving the benediction and holding a book in his left hand. The arch
of this compartment is pointed, while the others are
segmental. The space to the right of the centre is
occupied by the figure of a bishop or mitred abbot
giving the benediction with his right hand, while in
his left he holds the staff. The compartment to the
left of the central division contains a representation of
the Passion. There are figures of angels with censers
over each of the side arches. A border, within which
the whole is enclosed, is formed at the top and bottom
of a variety of fabulous animals; the sides represent
foliage, and in each angle there is a large rock crystal.
A fifth setting of crystal surrounded with smaller
gems occurs immediately over the figure which was
probably intended to represent St. Columba. The

sides and ends of the box are also richly chased. An
inscription in the Irish character upon the bottom
desires " a prayer for Cathbar O'Donell by whom the
cover was made," and for Sitric, the grandson of
Hugh, who made * * *.

The Caah appears to have been handed down from a
very early period in the O'Donell family, of which St.
Columba, the supposed writer of the manuscript which
it was made to enshrine, was a member.

The Domnach Airgid, also preserved in the Academy,
is perhaps the most precious relic of the kind under
notice now remaining in the country, as it contains,
beyond a doubt, a considerable portion of the copy of
the Holy Gospels which were used by St. Patrick during
his mission in Ireland, and which were presented by
him to St. Macarthen. Unfortunately the membranes
of which this singularly interesting manuscript is composed have, through the effects of time and neglect,
become firmly attached to each other ; but as several
have been successfully removed from the mass, it
is to be hoped that the whole may yet be examined.

Dr. Petrie, in a valuable Paper upon the Domnach
Airgid, published in the *Transactions* of the Royal
Irish Academy, has described the manuscript as
having three distinct covers: the first and most
ancient, of wood—yew ; the second of copper plated
with silver ; and the third of silver plated with gold.
The outer and least ancient cover possesses many
features in common with that of the Caah, though it
is probably of an age somewhat later. The plated

box enclosing the original wooden case is of very high antiquity.*

The Breac Maodhog.—This, which forms part of the Petrie Collection deposited in charge of the Academy, is one of the most curious of our ancient shrines. It is called after St. Maodhog, Moge, or Aidan, of Ferns, in the county of Wexford, and is most valuable on account of the details of ancient costume, ecclesiastical and military, which appear in connexion with certain castings or carvings attached to its sides.

There are in the Museum a considerable number of other shrines and ecclesiastical remains which should be examined by a stranger. This is, necessarily, but a sketchy survey, and one in which anything like an exhaustive description of the treasures referred to would be out of place.

Before leaving, visitors should see a number of swords and other weapons, found near Island-bridge, by labourers engaged in clearing ground upon which the terminus of the Great Southern and Western Railway now stands. Their preservation is not easily to be accounted for, unless it be shown that the earth in which they were found contains a peculiar anti-corrosive property, as although some bones were also found, their number was insufficient to warrant a supposition that their presence had in any remarkable degree affected the nature of the soil. The swords are long and straight, formed for cutting as well as thrusting, and terminate in points formed by rounding off the

* See *Transactions* of the Royal Irish Academy, vol. xx.

edge towards the back of the blade. The hilts are very remarkable in form, and in one or two instances are highly ornamented, as in the example here shewn. The mountings were generally of a kind of brass, but

several richly-plated with silver were found, and it is said that one of the swords had a hilt of solid gold. The spears are long and slender, and similar in form to the lance-heads used in some of our cavalry corps. The axe-heads are large and plain, and were fitted with wooden handles, which, as might be expected, have long since decayed. A number of iron knobs of a conical form, measuring in diameter about 4 inches, were also found. They are supposed to have been attached as bosses to wooden shields, of which they are the only remains.

All these weapons with one exception are composed of a soft kind of iron. Many of the swords were found doubled up, a circumstance for which it is difficult to assign a reason, as

Sword found at Kilmainham, Co. Dublin.

they had evidently been purposely bent. The sword represented in the engraving is remarkable for the unusual degree of ornament which appears upon its hilt, and also for its material, steel.

From several circumstances relative to the neighbourhood in which these remains were found, as well as from certain peculiarities in their form and character, our most judicious antiquaries have been almost unanimous in pronouncing them Scandinavian, and their opinion was fully borne out by that expressed by the celebrated Danish antiquary, Warsaac, during his visit to Dublin about the year 1848.

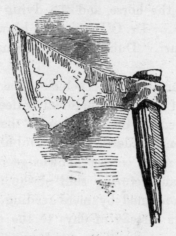

Axe-head from the Shannon.

Several axe-heads, discovered with many other antiques of various periods in the bed of the Shannon, and presented to the Academy by the Commissioners, are generally supposed to be Norman; but, they are quite as likely to have been used by the Irish, with whom the battle-axe was a favourite weapon.

Giraldus Cambrensis, in the reign of King John, thus speaks of the power with which the Irish of his time were wont to wield it :—" They hold the axe with one hand, not with both, the thumb being stretched along the handle, and directing the blow, from which neither the helmet erected into a cone can defend the head, nor the iron mail the rest of the body ; whence it happens that in our times the whole thigh (*coxa*) of a soldier, though ever so well cased in iron mail, is cut off by one blow of the axe, the thigh and the leg falling on one side of the horse, and the dying body on the other." Given by Dr. O'Donovan in his account of the battle of Clontarf, " Dublin Penny Journal," vol. i.

It may be remarked in conclusion that a few hours' examination of the truly national collection of antiquities preserved in the Museum of the Science and Art Department, Kildare-street, Dublin, will afford an inquirer a more correct knowledge of the genius, habits, and manufacturing skill of the ancient Irish, than may be obtained by mere reading, even should he devote years instead of days to the attainment of his object.

INDEX.

THE END.